SENSITIVE SKIN

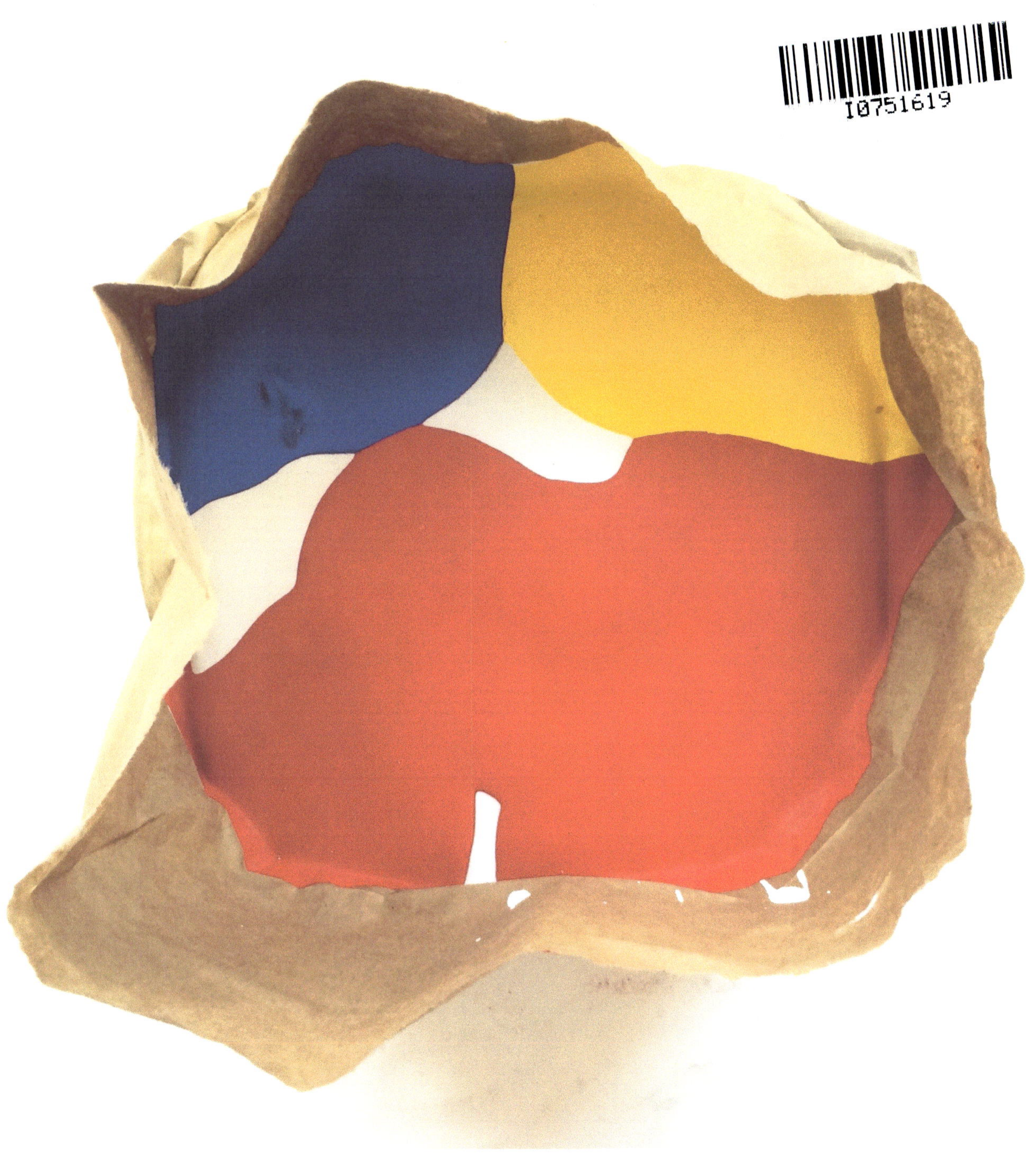

Sensitive Skin Magazine is also available online at
www.sensitiveskinmagazine.com.

Publisher/Managing Editor: Bernard Meisler
Editors: Rob Hardin, B. Kold, Steve Horowitz, Ron Kolm & Tim Beckett
Thanks to: Ron Richardson, Patrick O'Neil, Justine Frischmann, Jenny Wade and Franklin Mount

Front cover: *Paper Sack,* **10x10 inches (variable), Acrylic in paper bag, 2015 by Julie Torres**
Back cover: "Barking up the Wrong Tree (LIE)" © Winston Smith 2008, www.WinstonSmith.com.

You can find us at:
Facebook—**www.facebook.com/sensitiveskin**
Twitter—**www.twitter.com/sensitivemag**
YouTube—**www.youtube.com/sensitiveskintv**

We also publish in various electronic formats (Kindle, PDF, etc.), and have our own lines of books and recordings. For more info about **Sensitive Skin Books**, please go to
www.sensitiveskinmagazine.com/books/
and for **Sensitive Skin Music**, go to
www.sensitiveskinmagazine.com/downloads-store/.

To purchase back issues in printed or PDF format, go to
www.sensitiveskinmagazine.com/back-issues/.

You can contact us at **info@sensitiveskinmagazine.com**.

Submissions: **www.sensitiveskinmagazine.com/submissions**.

"Flack from Taylor" was originally published in Sensitive Skin #5, Vol. 1, 1994
"It Is Not Here on Earth What I Am Seeking" was originally published in Sensitive Skin #5, Vol. 1, 1994
"The Viewing" was originally published in Sensitive Skin #5, Vol. 1, 1994

ISBN-10: 099615700X
ISBN-13: 978-0-9961570-0-1

Contents

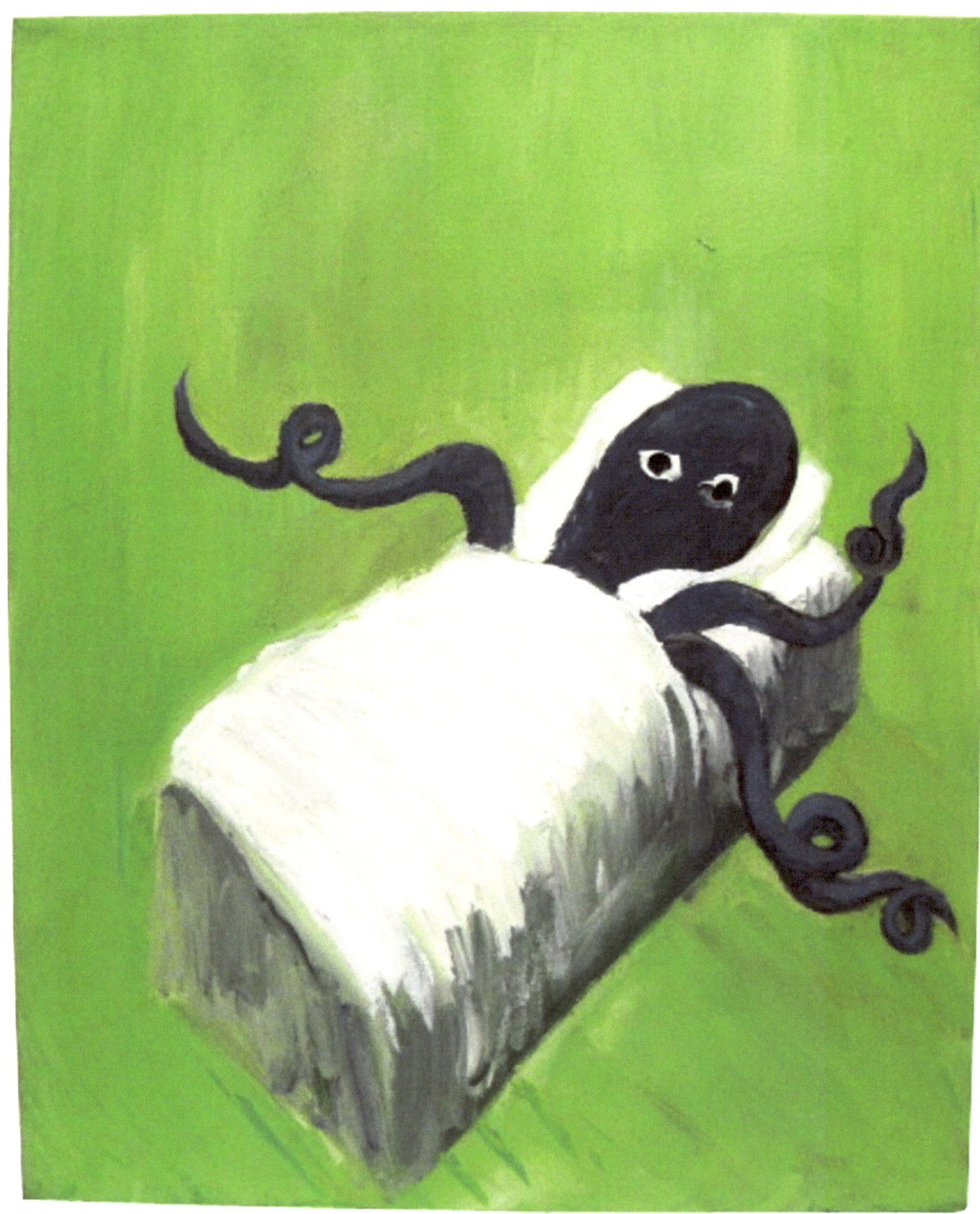

Quarantine, acrylic, 24" x 20", 2003 by Rick Prol

Owls

This Fuckin' Guy (as told to John S. Hall)

Owls don't seem so fucking wise to me.
They look like dicks, usually,
With their chests all puffed out and shit,
Like they're saying
"Fuck me? No—fuck you!"
But of course, they're not fucking saying that.

Owls don't actually want to fuck with you.
They will stay the fuck out of your way is what I've found.
But if you happen to be chipmunk running in a fucking field,
Or a squirrel fucking another squirrel, let's say,
And an owl sees you,
You're fucked.
You're fucked.

That fucking owl will swoop down on your chipmunk or squirrel ass
And pick you up with some sharp-ass motherfucking talons,
And fly you up to a branch,
And just fucking eat you.
Eat you alive.
That is some fucked up shit.

You could even be a fucking bird,
Just fucking flying along,
And that fucking owl will catch you in mid fucking air,
And you're fucked.
You're fucked.

Owls will also eat insects and fucking worms.
That doesn't seem so fucking wise to me.
I don't fucking know, but I mean,
The only time I ever ate a worm,
It was a worm at the bottom of a bottle of fucking tequila.
And that wasn't so fucking wise, let me fucking tell you.
I'm not saying owls are totally fucking stupid.
I'm just saying they're not fucking geniuses is all.

8/26/2014

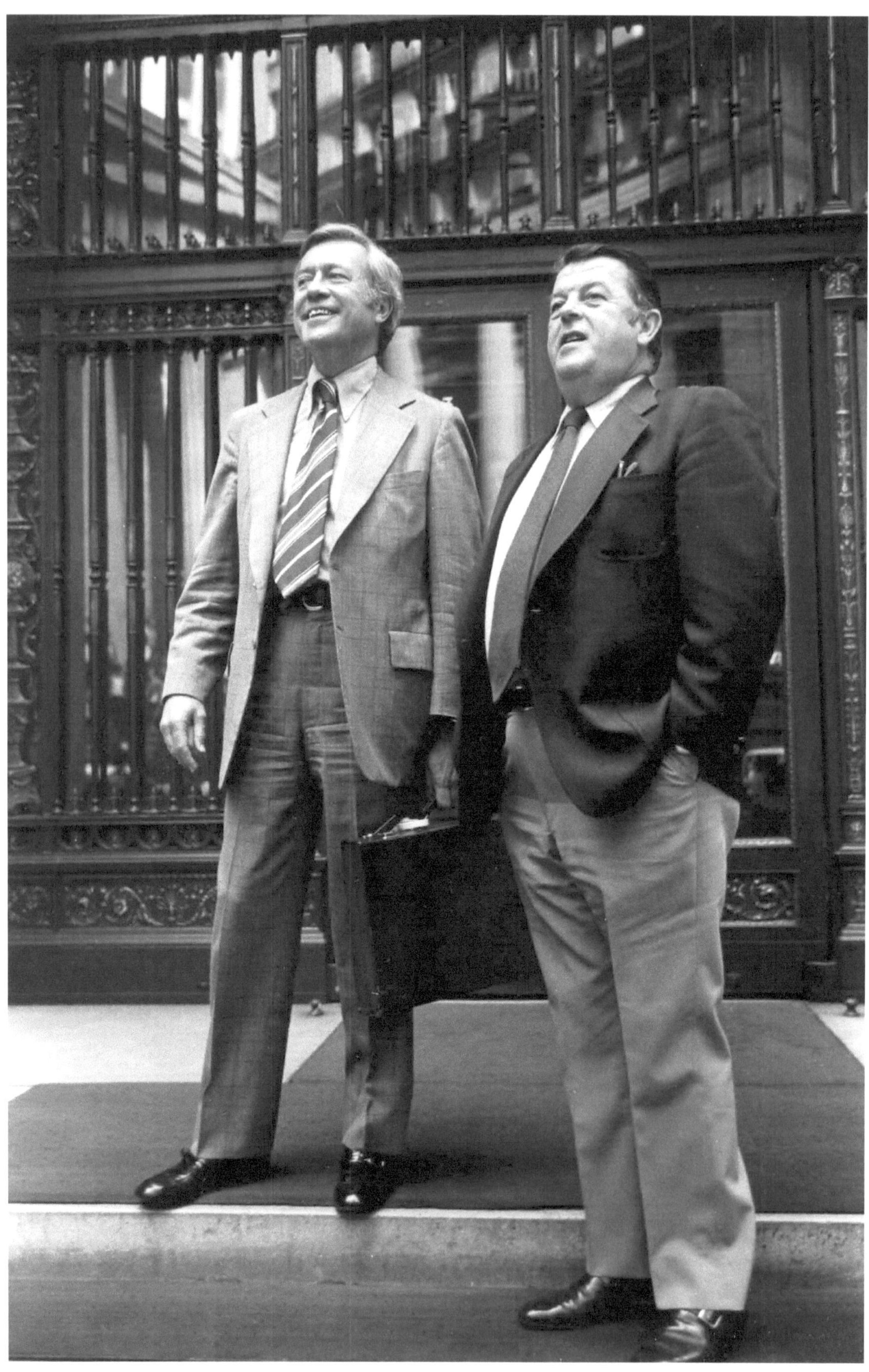

Photograph from the Wall Street series, by Charles Gatewood,

(10.1.13 will never come again.)

Bonny Finberg

Take the gas mask off. Take a bath.
Take the cake. Take the China exit.

Hell is out there too,
Other people's concern,
Gods' voices, at it like grownups
In the front seat.

Lunch tossed onto the flowers.
Who said you could take my blanket?
Cold hard cash—you promised.

A key must fit in some door or other.
No hard currency, yes,
Eyes in pockets, just a vacant glint.
The hand only grasps what it knows.

Everywhere is the sea,
This sea is everywhere.
This shit storm. This fancy death.

Remember being forgotten?
Can you?
Now forget remembering.
Bet you can't.
Even if you could,
Who would you tell?

Craving clouds,
Closing in on harebrained schemes,
What about the lawyers' fees?
The theft of tolls?
Who can tell?

The raisins big as plums,
Lines drawn across the water,
Never still for long,
Fish bait for the men who came and went,
Like parentheses.

Grass

JD King

(i love the scent
of fresh cut grass)

the mower is black
mostly
with bright orange
parts

no engine

to cut is to hear
the whir
of the reel
and to smell fresh cut
grass
in quivering air
insects rising

(i love the scent
of fresh cut grass)

crickets buzz
harbinger of autumn

attic dust
thick and soft
as a slice of bread

a fly's desiccated carcass lies
belly-up
on a window sill

she waves good morning
to the old couple whose doorstep
she pissed on last week
ignorant
they raise palms and smile
like idiots

midnight cabin
a woman
the window illuminated
blue

untie the string
lift the lid

a whisper of rainfall

(i love the scent
of fresh cut grass)

we got there
though I don't know how

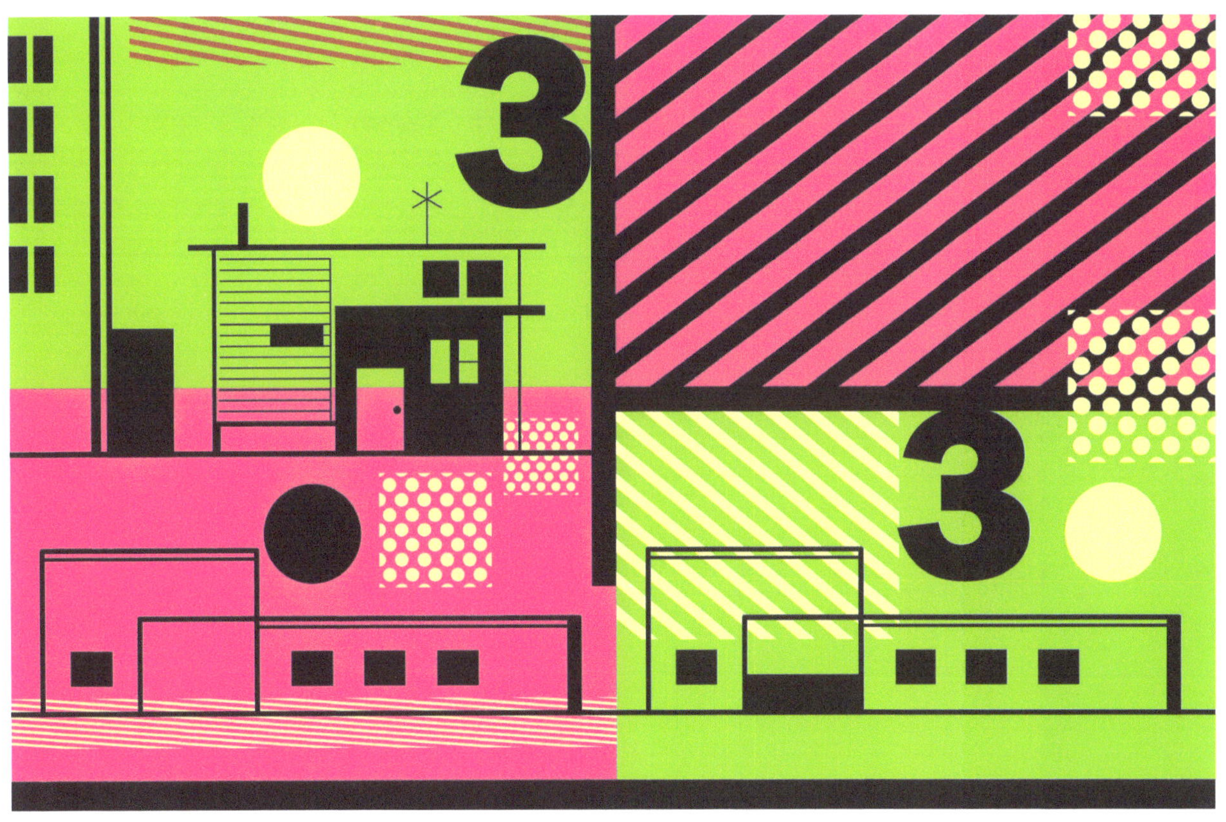

Illustration by JD King

justin hott at the airport

Emily XYZ

Justin Hott was a retail analyst for Bear Stearns I met at LaGuardia airport one night heading back to Detroit in December 2007, shortly before his company imploded.

What is the basis of greed / wanting to be free of money worries / There are 2 ways to do it: either you chase down money all your life / or you let go of the desire to be free of money worries / If you chase down money that springs the trap I'm pretty sure / Justin Hott at the airport hating life just wanting to be home with his wife and kid / but in too good a gig at that big building midtown Manhattan, woe, yeah / and as he said of Detroit: there's nothing for me there / meaning i cannot replace my golden salary in those dead boulevards, no way / Seven Mile Nine Mile Woodward whatever, you fuckin kidding me? / doesn't exist / So he was in the buddhist hell of the airport. How do religious people live? By charity / how do artists live? by charity / we are lucky / when someone comes to power who cares about religion or art / otherwise we struggle and die / altria, supporter of saints / bill and melinda the gateless gate / I would meditate more on this / but I should go look at the want ads

what am I missing? Persistence / fearlessness / which virtue on the self-empowerment list am I deficient in? check check check back, check back

I have a book of Zen stories / just one or two of these trust me are enough for enlightenment, and I have a whole book / and I would like another, bigger book, w/ more Zen stories / I study the Bhagavad Gita, a few lines of which will suffice for enlightenment / but I think of buying another translation, when I own 4 or 5 already / Any one page of Sri Nisargadatta, which I have been reading for years, would open the eyes of most people once and for all / but I consider buying all his books / I have a tape of Rudram sung by learned swamis carnatic perfection year in and year out I listen to these mantras but they bounce like arrows off a stone wall, and I think: I should get to the gym, I should get the new CD of Krishna Das / I have a whole roomful of keys, identical keys to the same door / but instead of opening the door, which any one would do / I buy the key again and again, and keep adding to the pile / so the question is / am I going to die in the cold and darkness outside the house / with a thousand copies of the key, unused, at my wanna-be lotus feet?

10 december 2007

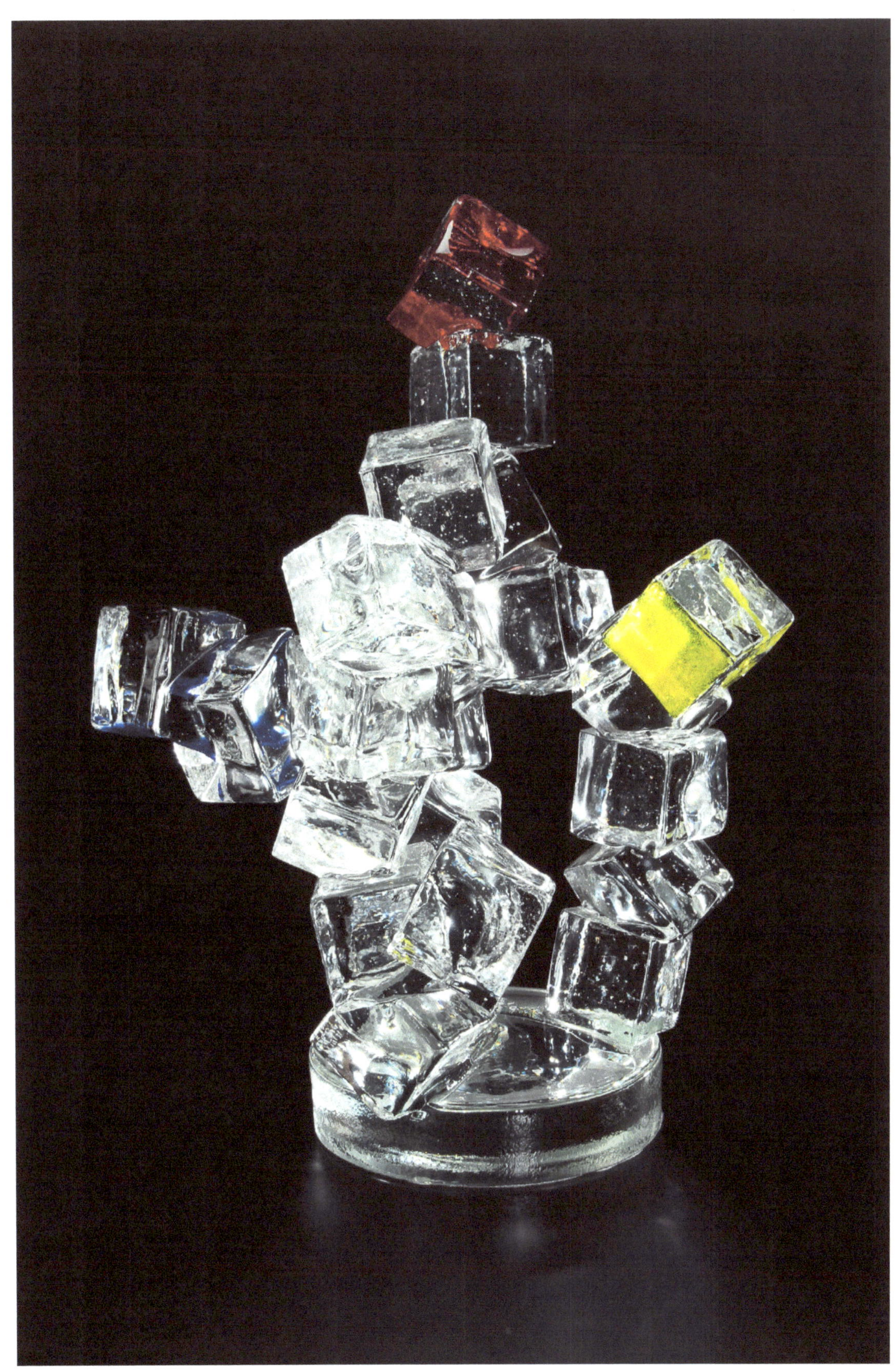

Sculpture by Henner Schröder

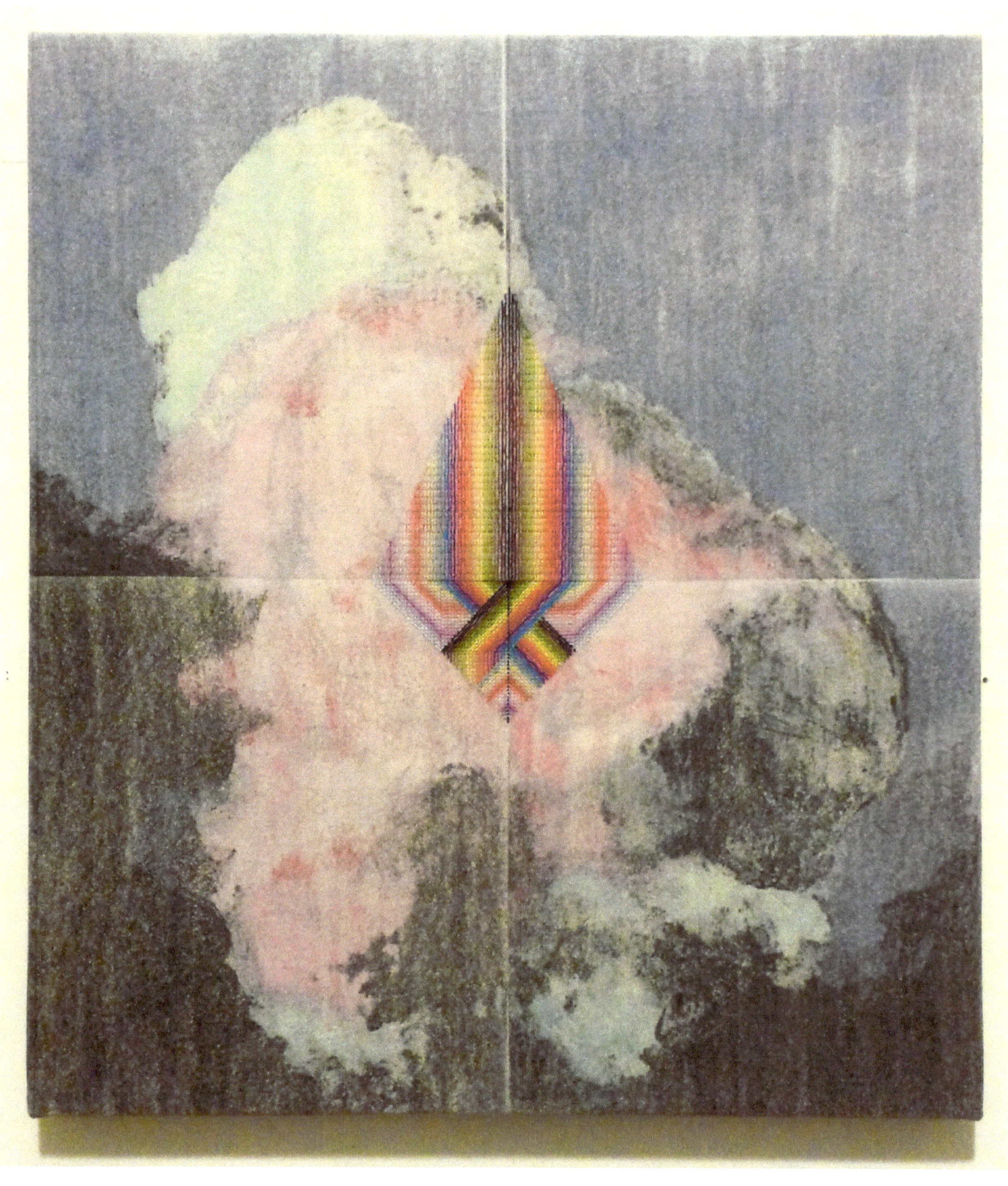

Diamond in the Sky, solvent transfer and cotton thread on canvas, 20" x 22", 2014, by Jonathan Cowan

Oakland

Marc Olmsted

Ocean fog thick in the avenue night
white Christmas lights in October
Shamrock Arms Bar
glowing green & red
through clear quartz-glass block front
the Dead Sailor Girls will play tomorrow
salt taste in air
where I'm a lost spirit
gliding over the rain-sheen streets
empty of cars & people

It Is Not Here on Earth What I Am Seeking

Jack Micheline

I don't know what I am seeking
In the cool night
rivers and birds
a sensuous lip
a rainbow of dreams
past waterfalls
the ruins of cities appear and fade in front of me
awkward man
he dresses and clowns
seeking love and shelter in criminal ways

I want to rip off the mask of the sniveling lip
from a want that runs
from an abstract pose
from a lie

This reality lies deep in the ground
or high in the sky
it is not here on earth what I am seeking
it is not in speeches or books
or in the heat of bedrooms or palaces or parties
it is not the dried heart or dead conscience of our age
it is somewhere that a child knows and is forgotten
it is an eye of a dog ravaged in streets
or in an open smile of a baker or shoemaker
it is by the fireside of rivers where men share bread and songs
that take my heart
and leave me limp and wobbly
drunk on eyes and feet and faces of the multitudes
I must travel to some far-off place
where rivers flow
and stars dance
where children bring garlands of love
and emeralds to the soft breeze of heaven
where prisons are not known
it is not here on earth what I am seeking
scavenged and torn bleeding from wars
and greed and shameless murders
let me just weep for the beauty I see and walk alone
to whatever dream and heaven I seek
then I will die with swans in the river
and send my love to strangers and friends
this poetry I breathe which is life and my heart
and to you who seek the unknown
I send you love and the rivers

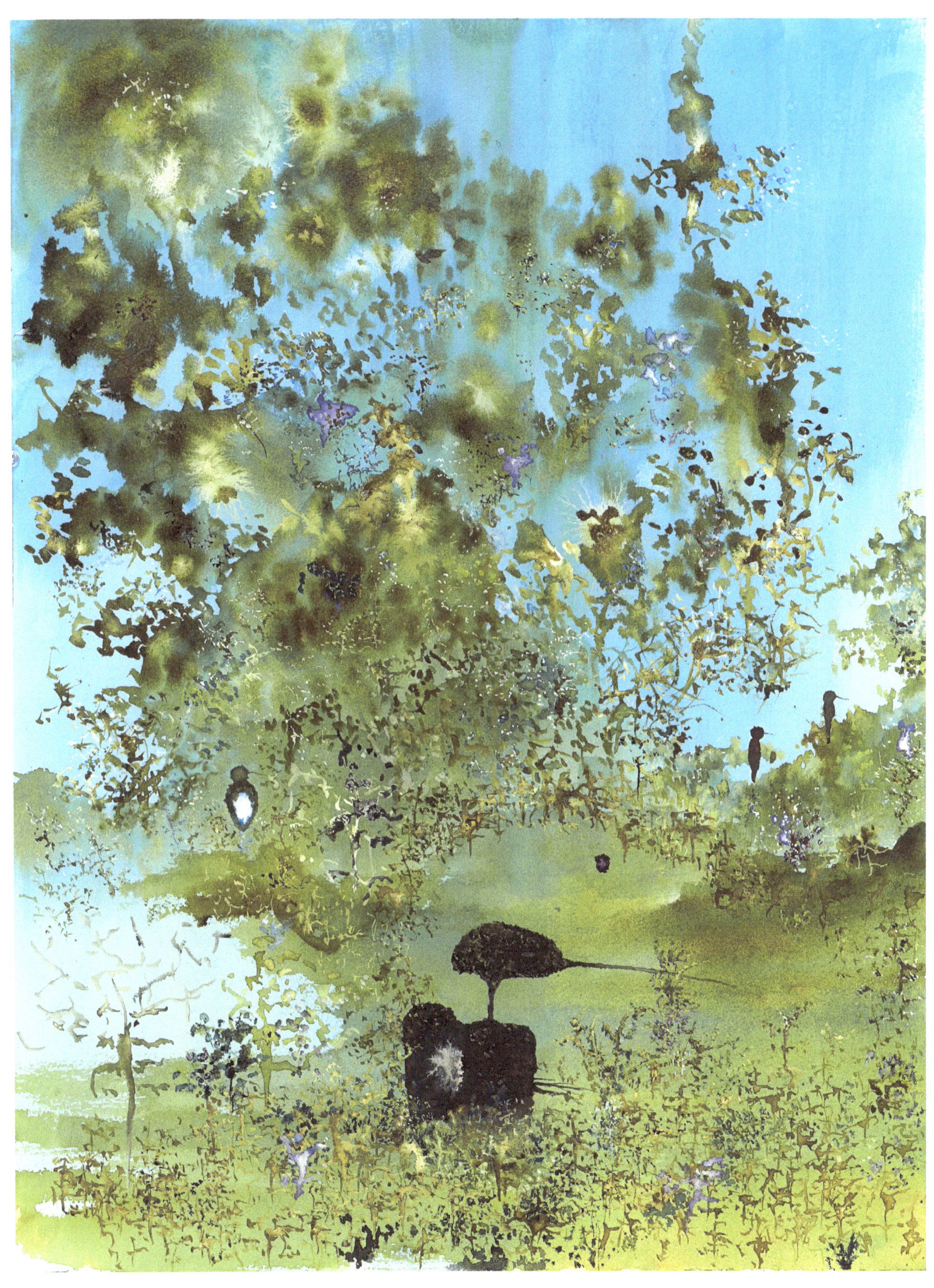

I can't get chikungunya because it's called chikungunya, watercolor on paper, 2014, by John Lurie

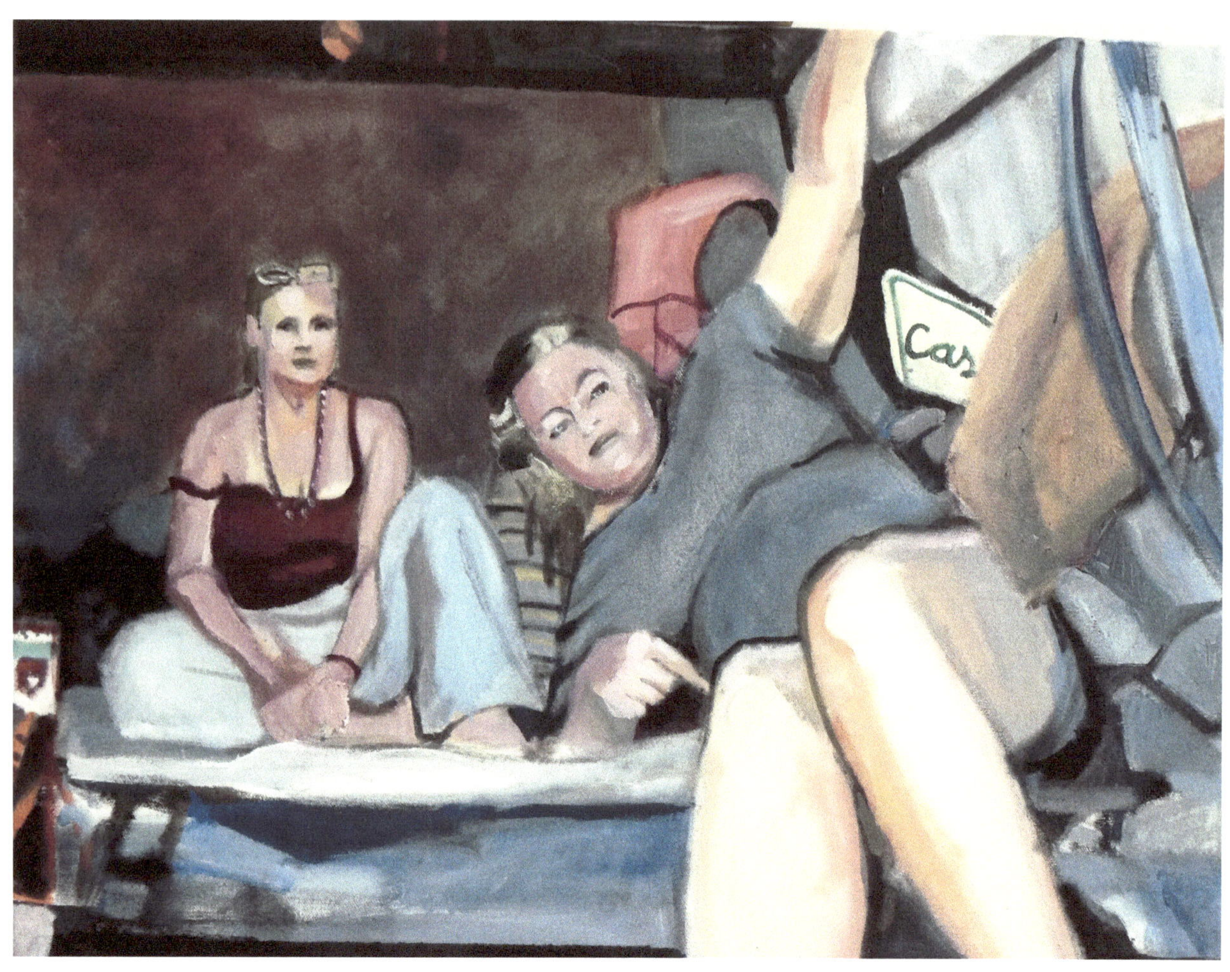

Ladies of the LAX Parking Lot, oil on canvas, 22" x 17", by Liz Kresch

Our Heavy Metal Life

Jose Padua

Sometimes I like to imagine that my family
and I are a heavy metal band,
playing gigs in the southern states,
riding in a big tour bus that has skulls
painted on the side,
and a big decal of the grim reaper
wielding his scythe
on the rear windshield,
moving east on Interstate-40
out of Nashville,
still hungover but blasting the stereo anyway,
and hearing songs about leather jackets
and chains and drinking Jack Daniel's
from a groupie's shiny black boot.
I'm the singer and I play bass,
my wife's the main songwriter
and plays rhythm guitar,
and my daughter shreds wickedly
on the lead guitar
while my son pounds the drums
like an animal in a zoo about to rip apart
the bars of its cage.
This is what weekends are like
for us—we keep moving until we get tired
because we're on a mission
that's best measured in decibels.
The songs we play will make you bang
your heavy heads.
You will rise before us,
our faithful minions,
like power chords from the rough mix,
and when we get home
we stick the leftover casserole
in the oven
then feast upon it,
because we are vicious birds of prey,
and every time I walk into the kitchen
I shake my fist and grimace because the dirt
on our floor is black.

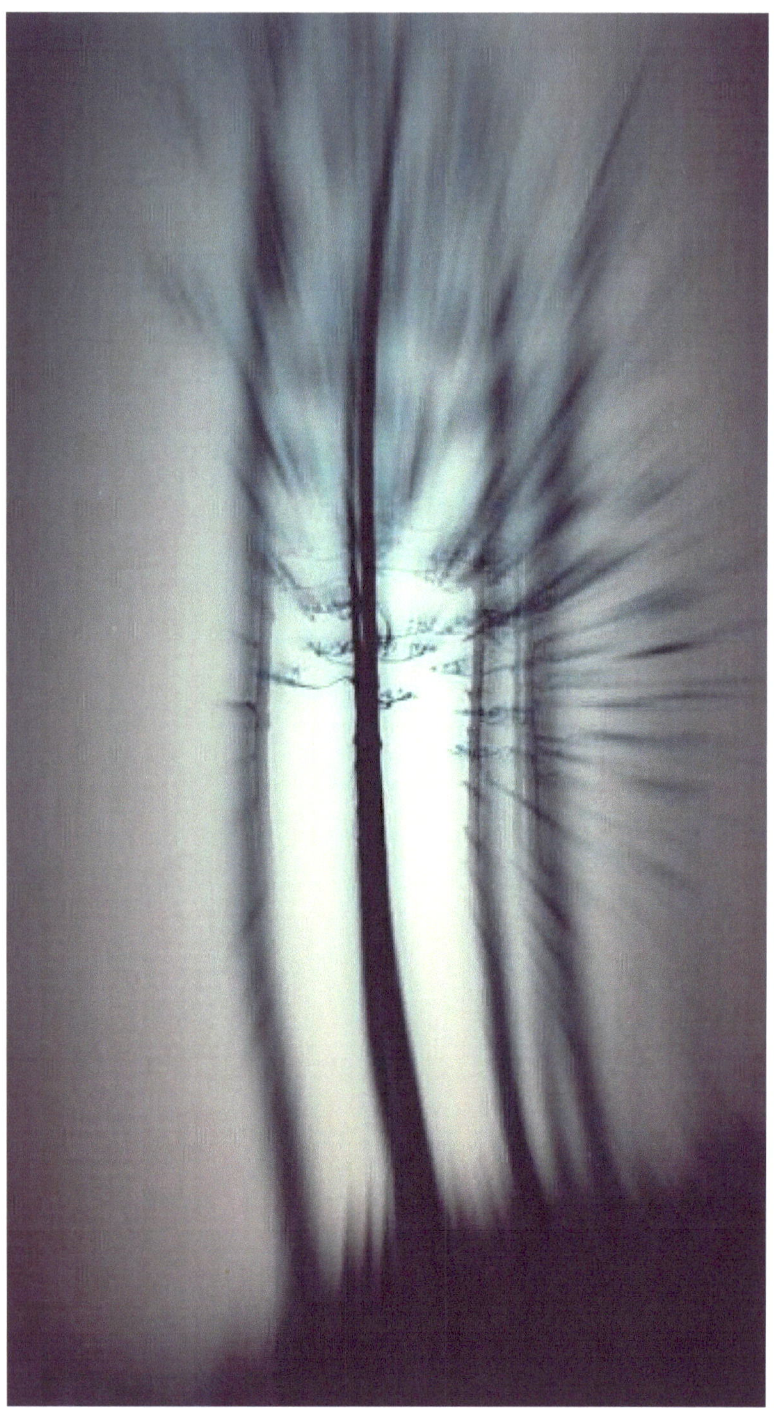

Photograph by Kym Ghee

In General

Michael Randall

My friends tend to laugh when I bare my soul
and slowly nod when I tell a joke

These things occur to me only when I'm high
and might have no truth whatsoever

I'm most honest when purely drunk
yet somehow pure belief still eludes me

Strange how my worst lies are the most believable
since I tend to succeed at that which interests me least

Sacred cows give milk to the poor
and the poor throw up on their shoes

if they're lucky and then of course
clouds have more ambition than I want

8th Street Station (Yin-Yang)

Ron Kolm

I met you
At the Grey Gallery
Across from Washington Square Park.
We were going to the opening
Of *The Left Front: Radical*
Art in the "Red Decade."

We ate all the peanuts
And most of the chips
That were set out as snacks,
And drank way too much wine
Which seemed to annoy the NYU
Students who were serving us.
They gave us dirty looks
But didn't actually
Say anything.

I left you and walked
Over to Broadway
To get an R Train home
Still pretty buzzed.

Inside the station
I went to the downtown end
Like I always do
To sit on the wooden bin
That's been there for years.
But this time I couldn't—
It was covered with trash
So I stood on the platform
And waited for a train.

A razor-thin tranny
Sporting a long blonde wig,
Nose ring and high-heeled boots
Walked over to the mess,
Glared at it, then furiously
Swept it away with her hands
Flinging Styrofoam cups
And sandwich wrappers
At everyone
Standing nearby.
I didn't mean to stare
But her sudden rage
Took me by surprise.

"Don't look at me, bitch!" she screamed.
"Do you want to get pushed
In front of a train
And die?"

She yanked a bottle
From her jacket pocket
And smashed it against the wall,
Just like in the movies,
Spraying glass everywhere
And dared me to attack her.
I looked in my bag
For my umbrella
Which I figured
I'd use as a weapon
If I had to.

Just then a train pulled into the station--
I got on, turned and shouted:
"I was on the wrestling team
In high school . . ."
But I couldn't finish the sentence
Before the doors closed.

I looked out the window
As the train left the station
And saw her sitting
On the wooden bin
Lighting a cigarette.

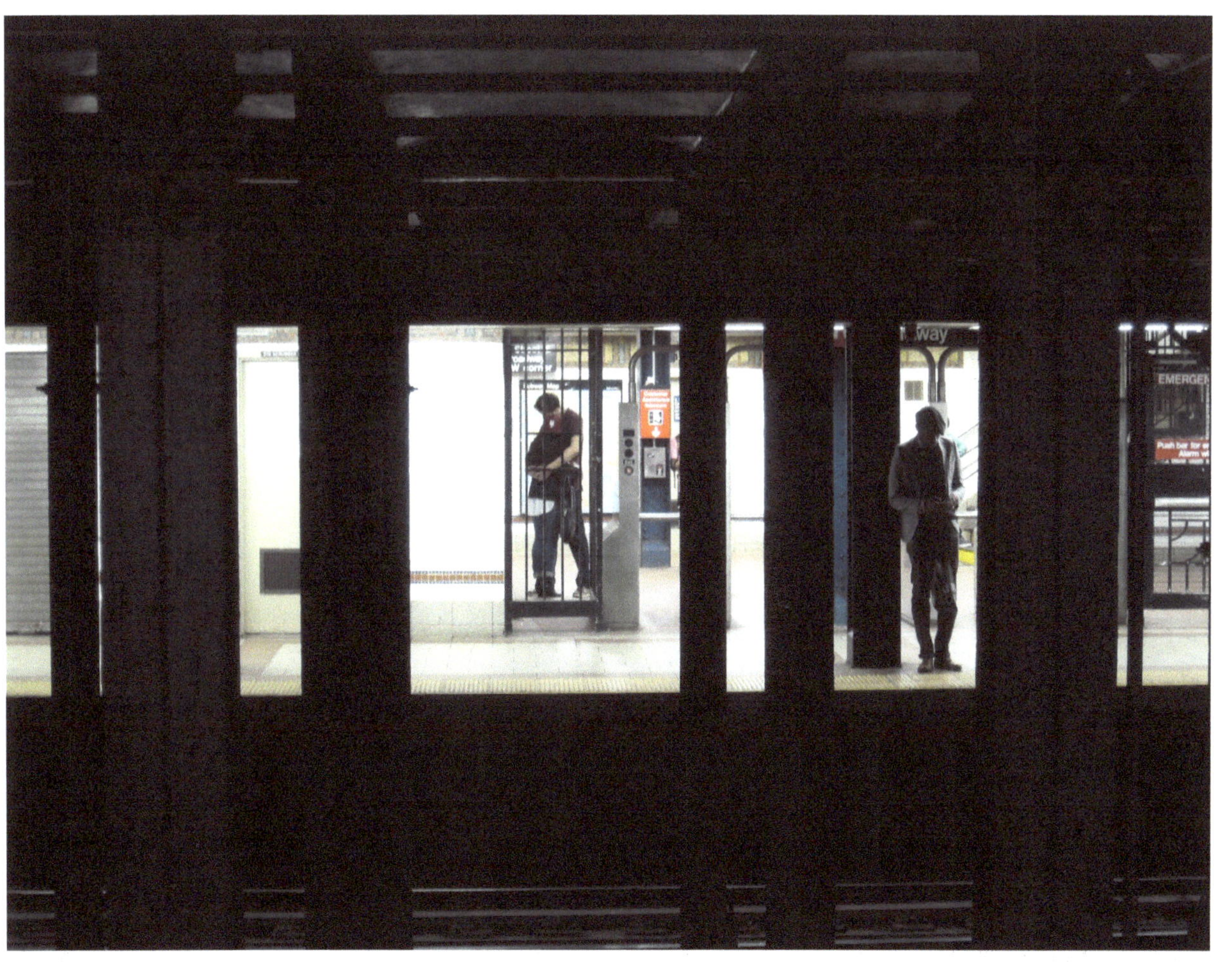

Photograph by Daniel Kolm

What Friends Say

Pete Simonelli

Jason moved across the floor on his hands and knees,
I see him this way constantly, in that scooting motion,
making his way to the records lined against the other wall.
Dawn is lighting up outside. He says,

"You have to know what you mean
before you mean what you say."

He was always handing down these admonitions
while flipping through records, high on dope
and curiosity at the same time, in that infant addict stage.
He couldn't be bothered
with what he hadn't deduced on his own.

In the hospital, his father told him to pull the plug,
and he did it. End of story.
It's not just anyone who can be troubled.
I for one am not guilty today, I said,
I'm only singing.

Years later, on the day Jack Gilbert died, word came
that our apartment would have to be vacated.

I listened to Gilbert's reedy, able voice
reading poem after poem and, frankly, didn't feel much better,
just more enlightened: the Jewish women at Dachau pushing out the Nazi guard
who wanted to die with them and singing
"for a little while" after the chamber door closed.

Under dull skies of November,
I see Jason, long dead now, turn,

after the flowers have just gone, the fleeting
architectures of a world just past that refuses

to place blame on anyone
and exists only for a peculiar sort of genius

made of misery & anger. Even Spring, singing,
blows down its roses

and the buds crumple down upon
a conclusion in which they too have no say, saying

suns come up, rains bristle the rivers, winds chop
the big bodies of water, suns go down again.

And moons, like women, like Jason, if you're lucky, pop up at weird moments
athwart buildings, mirrored in car windows, looking

at you within reach, offering so much light
they cancel light.

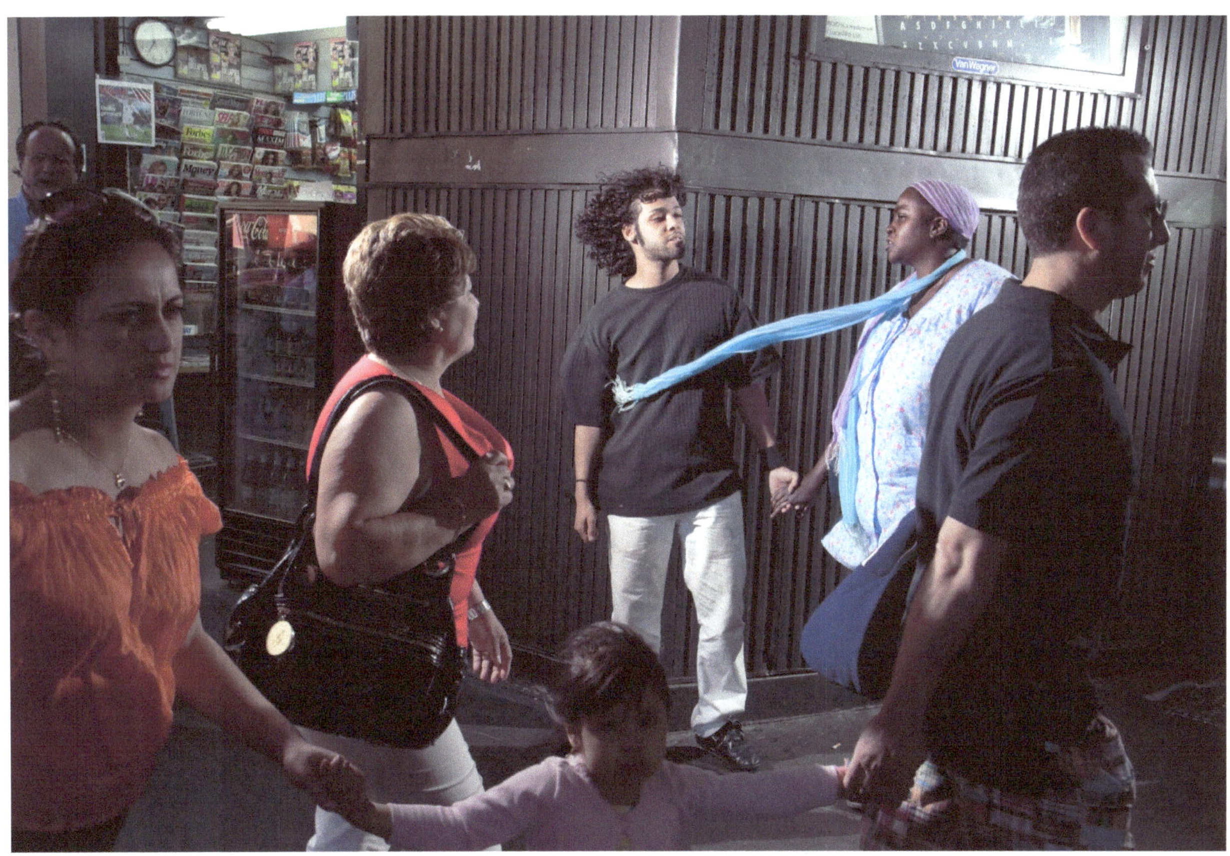

Photograph by Jean-Christian Bourcart

Sing This One Back to Me

Bob Holman

Honeybee honeybee deep in the honeytree
Do not tell me to suck dry the tips of whip grass
Swan sway swan sway Ganges flows all day
Would you send me off then to the blasting seas?
Tale singer nightingale crooner carousing on the leaf drip
Who dares say, Excuse me, quiet please, eat dry leaf clippings
This robin rocking tail lit by the fullest moon
Try to redirect to fogbound swirl, see what happens to you
My feet on the lotus? No, my feet *are* the lotus!
All God? Gosh, I was looking over at you – shh.
No need this talking, this poem so obvious, shh.
Sing this one back to me

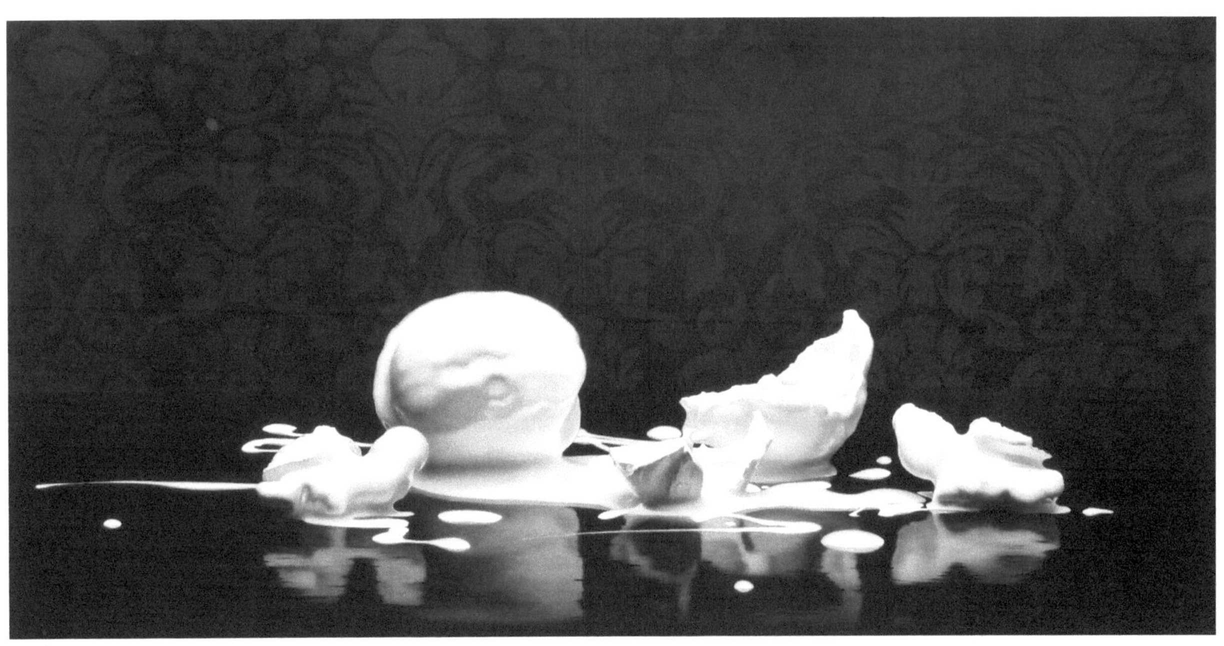

#111 Dripping Memory Series—Walnuts, oil on linen, 2013, by David de Biasio

Other Body Parts Are Worthy of Attention

Hal Sirowitz

"My problem is I'm both attracted and repelled by the male organ."
—Diane Keaton, *Manhattan*

I hope you don't quote me
as saying I like your sexual organ,
she said. There are better things

I'd like to be known for - like
being a good listener. I don't
have a special relationship

with only one part of your
body. I relate to every part,
even your eardrums. It's hard

for me to not notice your groin
at times, but I hope to spend
equal time with your other

body parts, like your heels.
It's difficult to say, "Put your
heels on my lap." You might

come away thinking I have
a foot fetish. You'd be
dreadfully wrong.

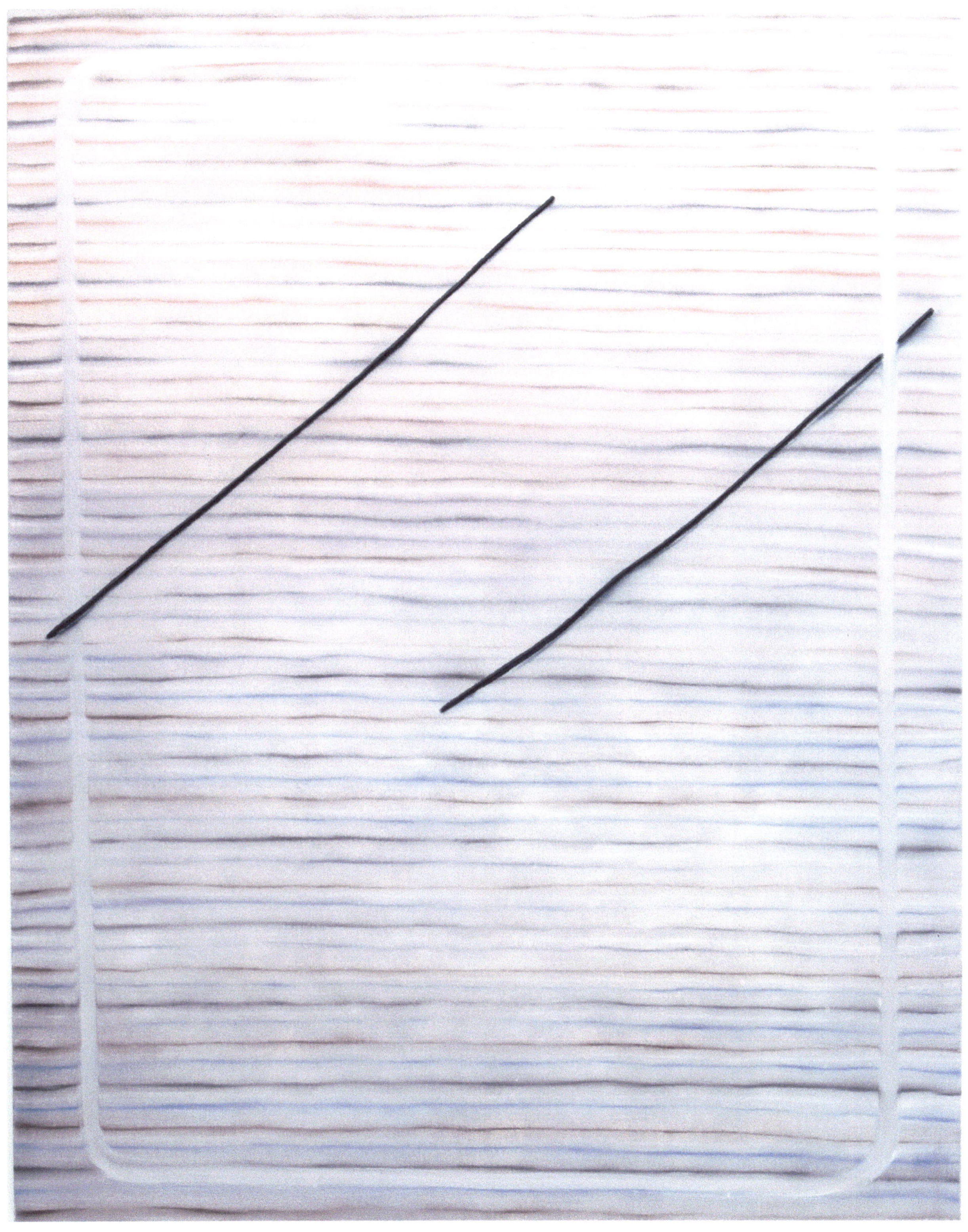

Soft break up, oil on linen, 64" x 50" , 2014, by Clinton King

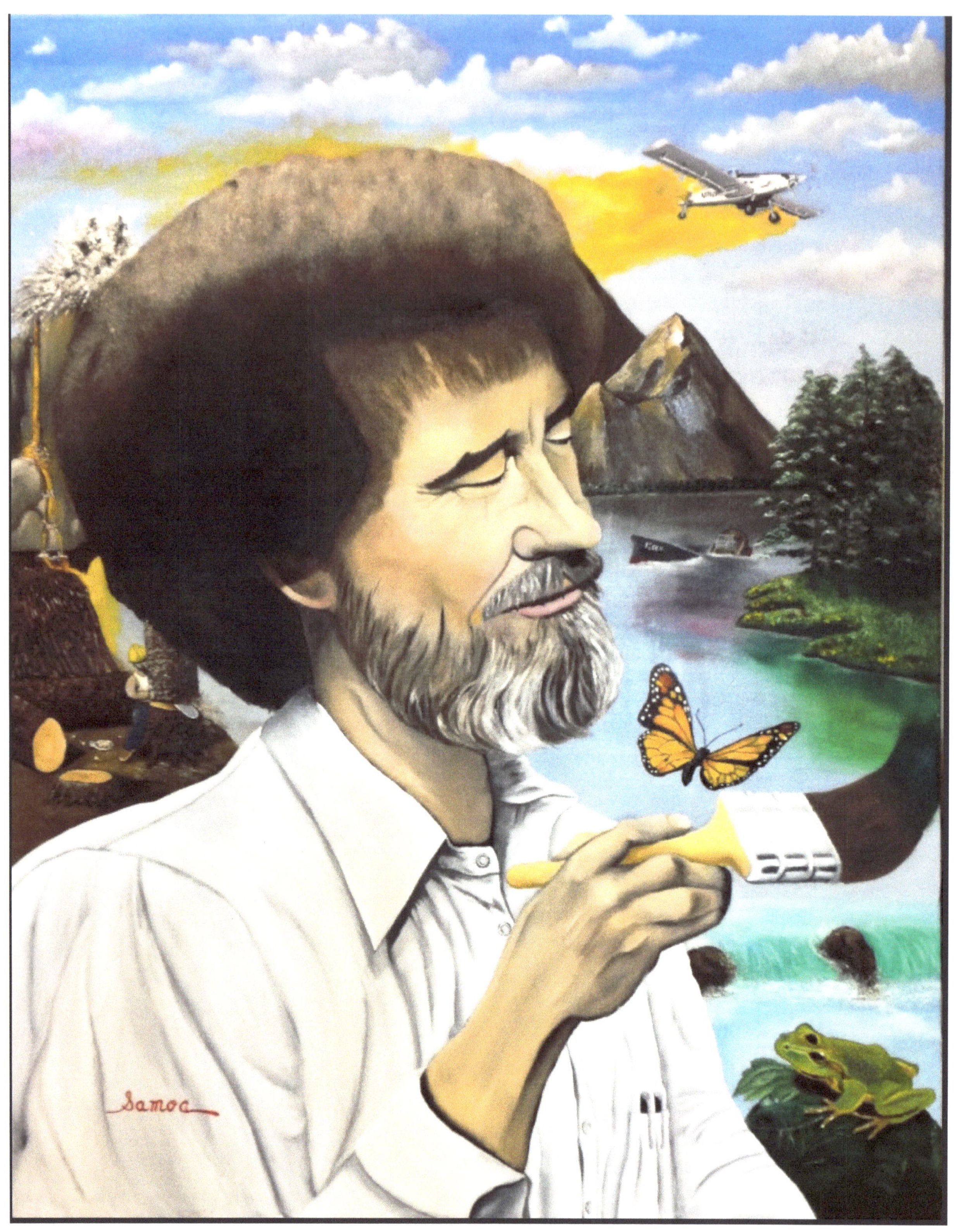

Bob Ross, oil on canvas, 24" x 30", 2014 by Samoa Moriki

Poetry Toys

Sparrow

Yes,
there
are
bobble-
head
dolls
of
Poe,
but
where
are the
action
figures
of
Auden?

the perfect child

steve dalachinsky

i am a descendant of those that have survived for centuries
& my mother wanted me to be the perfect child
i am still amazed that people know how to make doors
their ingenuity baffles me
way beyond that of a beaver & its dam
a beehive full of hungry workers
an ant colony
or a violent dream

crossing guards bear witness
where the vision of others fails
this is the basis for massive liquidity
a mitigation pushed to its cause
liquidity: the way a tour begins
a short speech perhaps before the walk begins
i am in awe of the fact that towns are summoned
from dust
buildings are erected
cities born
bottles of liquidity / high picon light
within passages of long narrow space
the sudden insistent tickling of an alarm
on the clock's worn face
in a dark pocket
it never happened before
this act as natural as the body behind me
that breathes down my neck
i will be your tour guide
as you walk between these shadows
we so fondly cling to
yet so often forget are there
INCREDIBLE that they are there don't you think?

i am still amazed by breath or is that: at BREATH?
the action of breath / breathing
the very motion of its invisibility
one of the best pieces of instance i have ever heard
for instance the CIRCLE begins HERE opens here
SWOOPS
when a bargain @ any price begun
as in BE OUR TOUR
an avenue full of DENSE / Ness

i want so much to be this PERFECT CHILD
its purpose A GUIDE - i want to walk to guide you
to take your hand – house you but maybe not feed & cloth you
as the MOTTO goes: spill your beings - all 2 of you – en masse
massive YOUS & that perfectly rounded naked shoulder
as if blushing in the pale red light
the black thin strap / holding the hatting
breeze on my back the hatting breeze - the sticky liquid beneath my chin
these massive bodies > la jolla in it the gravity of a circle
the circle that begins begets or price jam let me bond overdosing itself
write about like a tour you sometimes take thru this dark room
on bright avenue or a shallow light spilling into your glass like an unpainted city

have no fear i am a perfect, far from perfect child – so let me be your tour guide
let me guide you on this tour this breeze a breeze where does it come from
this BREEZE ????

completed 11/6/14 3 fragments from 10 & 11/14

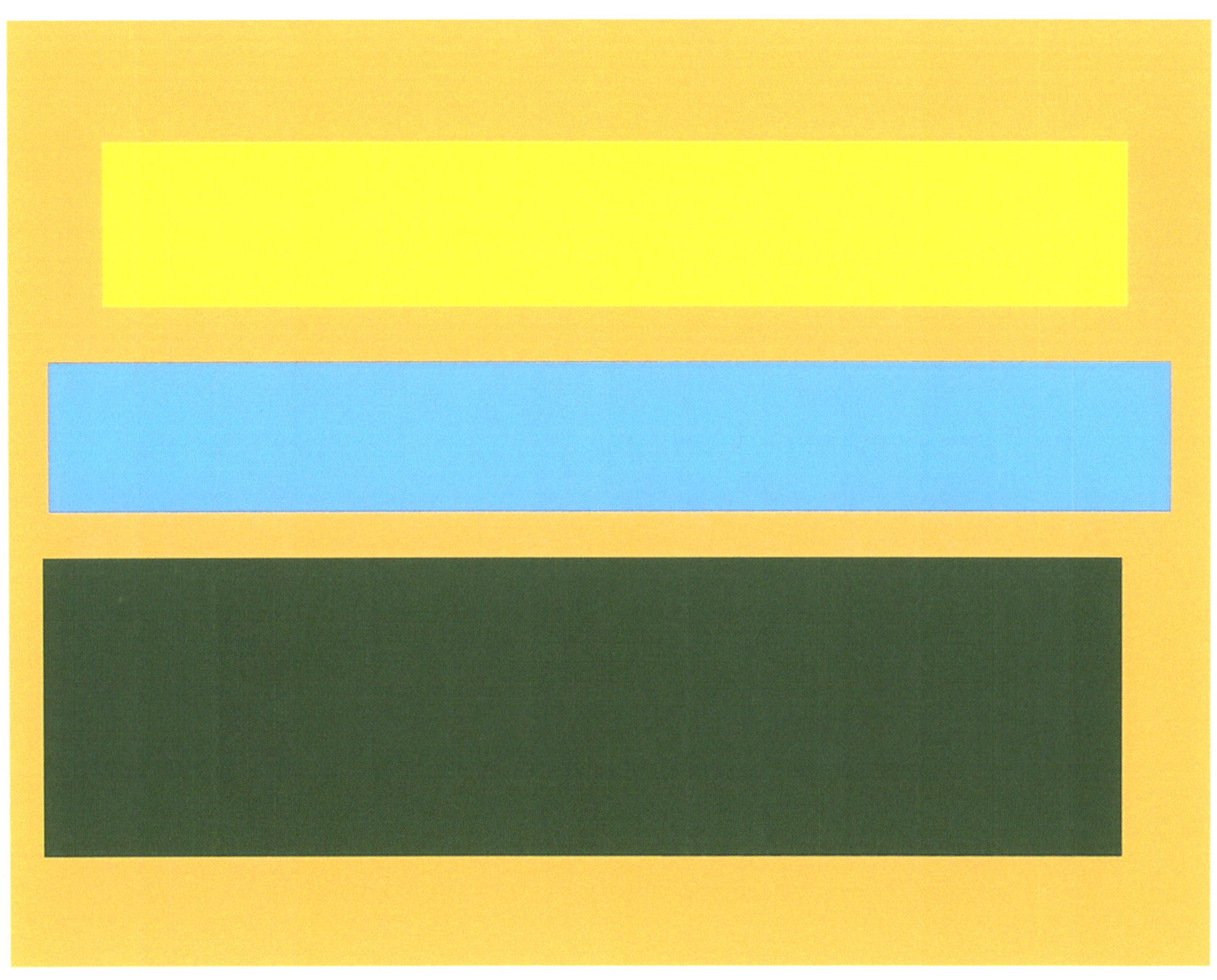

Terra-Haute, acrylic gouache on panel, 2012, by Tom McGlynn

Swallow the Evidence

Wanda Phipps

Inspired by *The Limits of Control*, a film by Jim Jarmusch

my mind hops back
to the century trees
of Cabo de Gata
a woman in platinum wig
white cowboy hat
white trench coat
and cowboy boots
covered in leopard's skin
strides through the nearly
mud-like surface
folding the earth
with her heels and
counting the flamingoes
as she goes
she whispers to me
in a stern chastising voice
"you must remember
your lines!" then I see
myself onstage freezing
forgetting "going up"
as she wanders up
cobblestones going up
and up and up the
winding Spanish streets

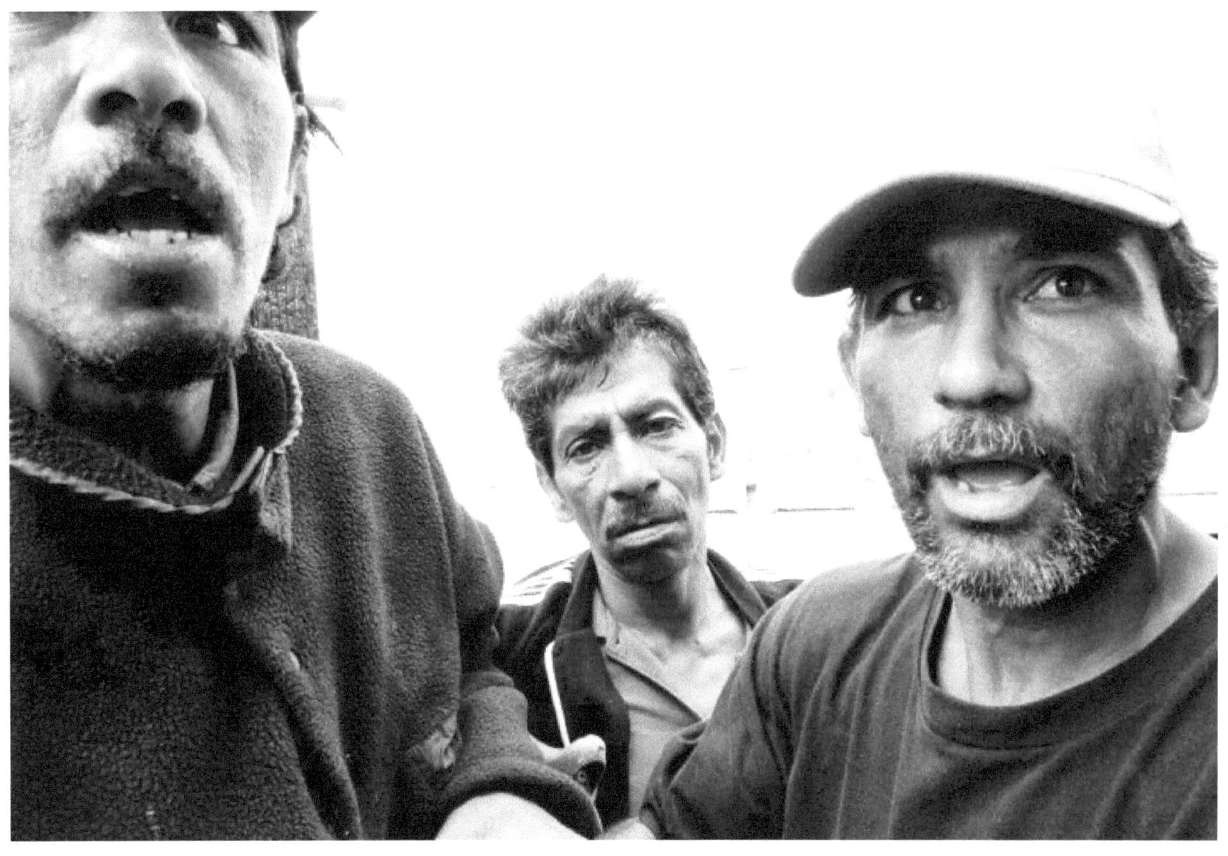

Photograph by Chris Bava

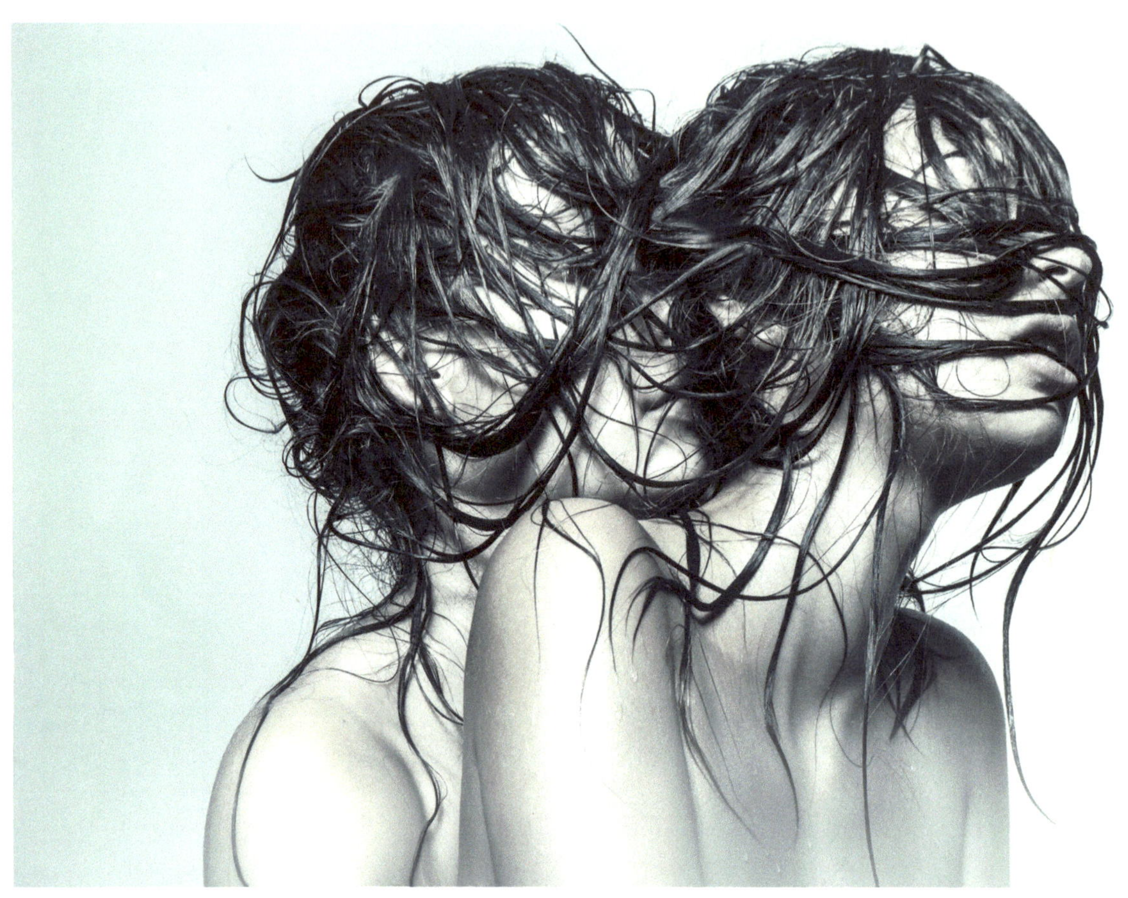

Metamorphosis, photograph, by Evelyn Bencicova

Linda

Eddie Woods

LINDA

"songs like a practiced whore
who turns away from no one
but the one who loves her."

Djuna Barnes

How deathly strange it all seems—
especially here on the thin edge of passion,
where all eyes chilled into beauty
in blind innocence shield themselves
against the night rain of reality;
how strange what a worldliness of difference,
even at our ages of man,
one simple kiss makes between two people
who never before that soft moment touched their lips
knew how much sorrow they had in common
or how much joy.

Of the "10,000" girls I've seen standing on street corners,
whose hard eyes like yours warned me into caution,
until then you were the least of images
my groin might have warmed to
or the catholicity of my faith
recognized as the purity I feel you are.

It is whores like you,
with all your feigned deceptions,
who time after time prove beyond question
the perfumed existence of that stunning black hole
known to mystics as God.

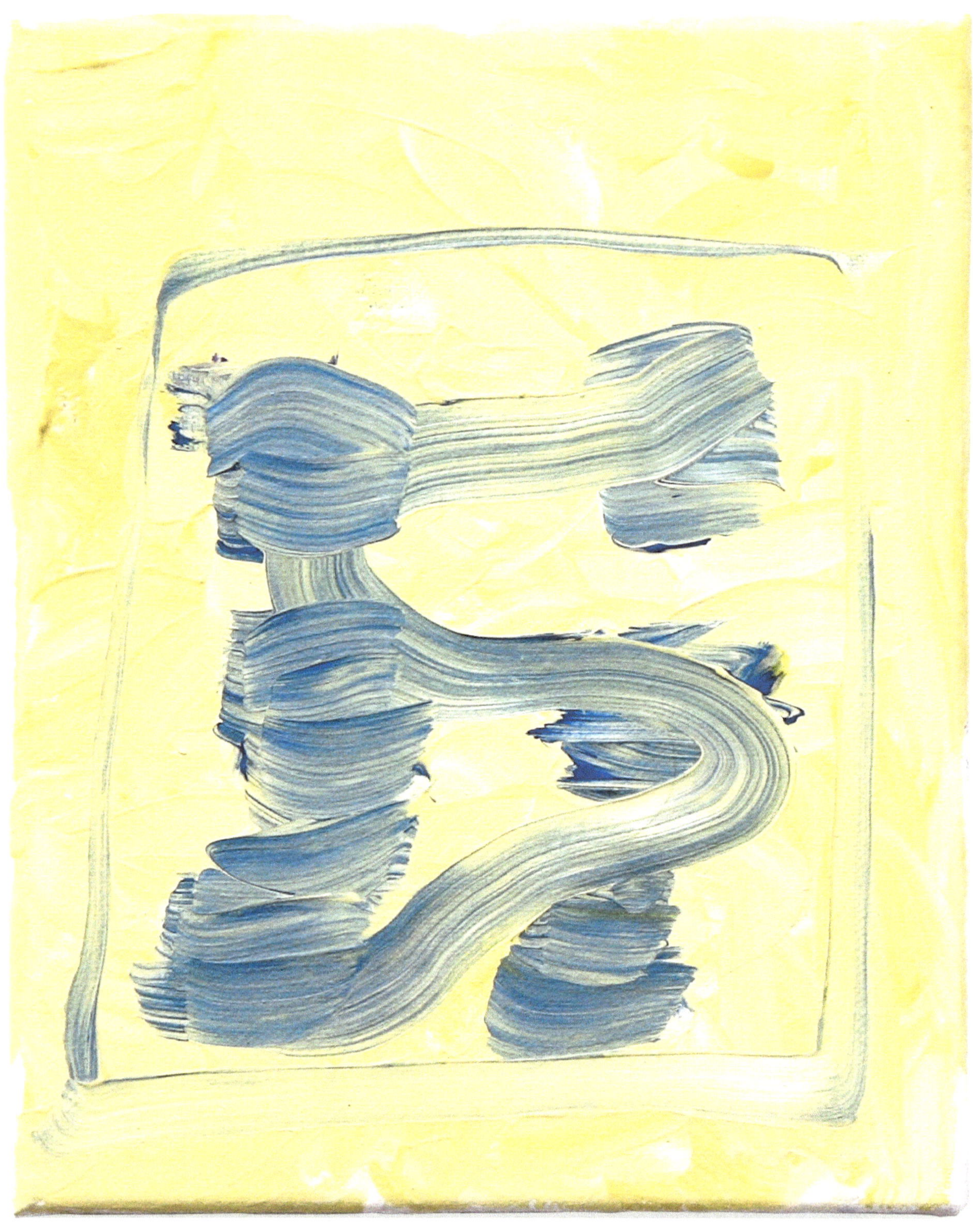

Untitled, acrylic on canvas, 10" x 8" , 2014, by Peter Shear

Some of My Friends

Max Blagg

"Some of my friends don't know who they belong to."

Dipsomanic daytrippers kicking it
in small motels on desert mornings
dancing a june bug sonata
percussive staccato legato
flowing smooth and certain as a river
Gram Parsons wailing through the walls
infinity blue skies
emptiness surrounding emptiness
storm light orange as a flagman's vest
Chet Baker had it coming
they punched his lights out in Dusseldorf
then tossed him from a window in Amsterdam
he landed on a concrete blond and was gone
along with all the other forms
of beauty he used to conjure,
sexy junky sadism fading
behind his slowly glazing eyes.

The boom boom room of guilt and regret
remains open 24/7 so sip supersize
cokes at the 7/11 until you are
too wide to get in your vin diesel vehicle
and yet thine eyes have seen the glory
of the knees bent show a leg ecstatic
configurations recalling Indian temple walls
limbs parting slow as diamonds
descending through glycerine
raising the head to god's gate again
creamy as the foam
on your five dollar coffee,
hoping the thought police
won't find you here
soaking in your degradation
reading Thomas Merton
in an attempt at redemption
before the night shift arrives
and tosses your hair dryer
into the bathtub.

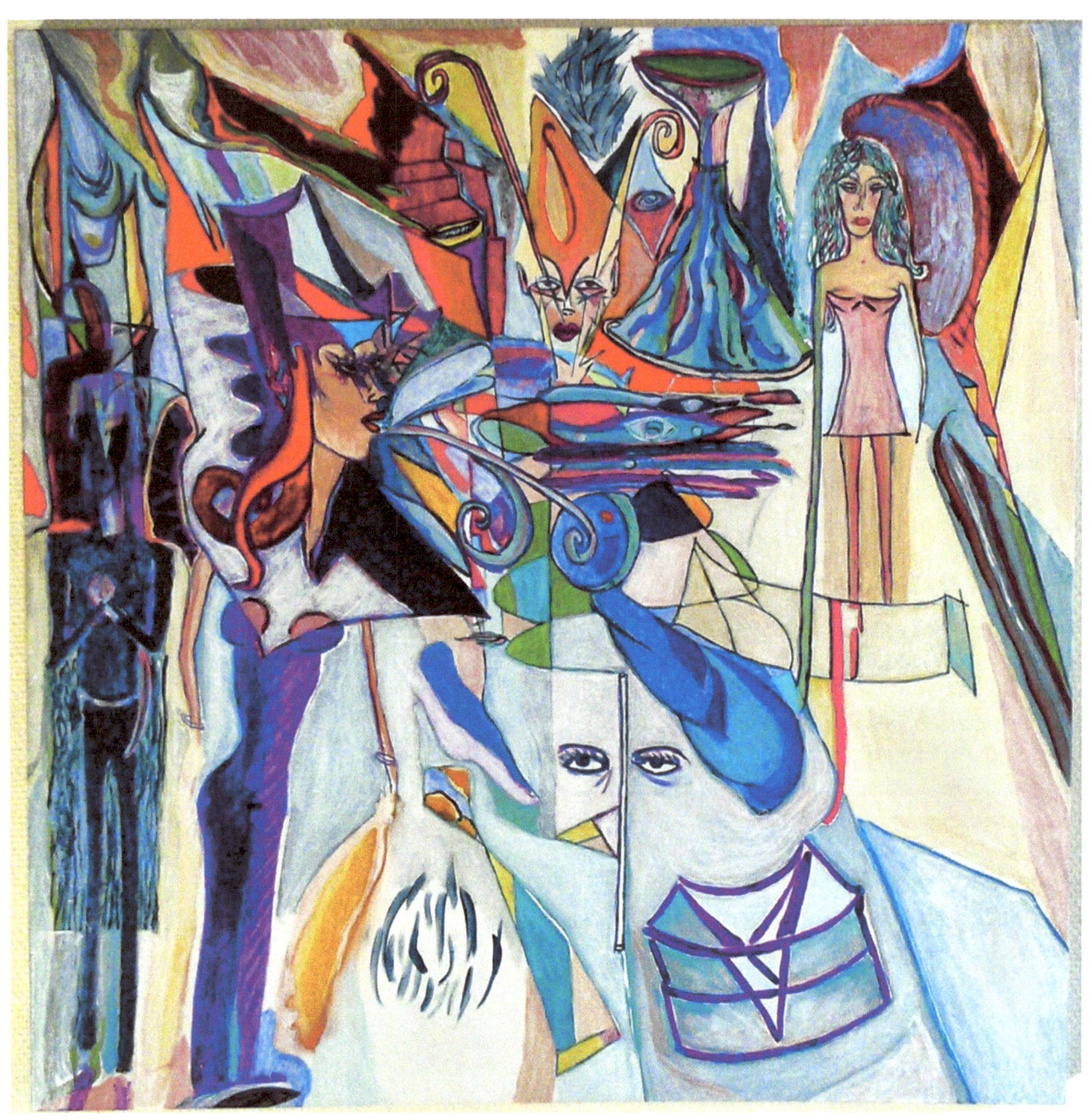

'A Psychedelic Representiation of my Lack of Skills either Understanding or Communicating Normally,
acrylic and vinyl on canvas, 80cm x 80cm, 2013-14, by David West

Erasure, The Lotus Eaters, Ulysses*

Larissa Shmailo

BY LORRIES ALONG SIR JOHN ROGERSON'S QUAY
past Nichols' the undertaker's. Eleven, daresay.
Sent his right hand with slow grace over his hair:
Where was the chap I saw in that picture somewhere?
Ah, in the dead sea, floating on his back;
It's a law like that. Curriculum. Crack.
It's the force of gravity of the earth is the weight.
Per second, per second. Post office. Too late.
Eleven, is it? I only heard it last night.
What's wrong with him? Dead. And, he filled up, all right.
Chloroform. Laudanum. Sleeping draughts. Phlegm.
Better leave him the paper and get shut of him.

* Lines in this found poem are taken in exact order and sequence from the "Lotus Eaters" episode of *Ulysses* by James Joyce, with intervening material erased.

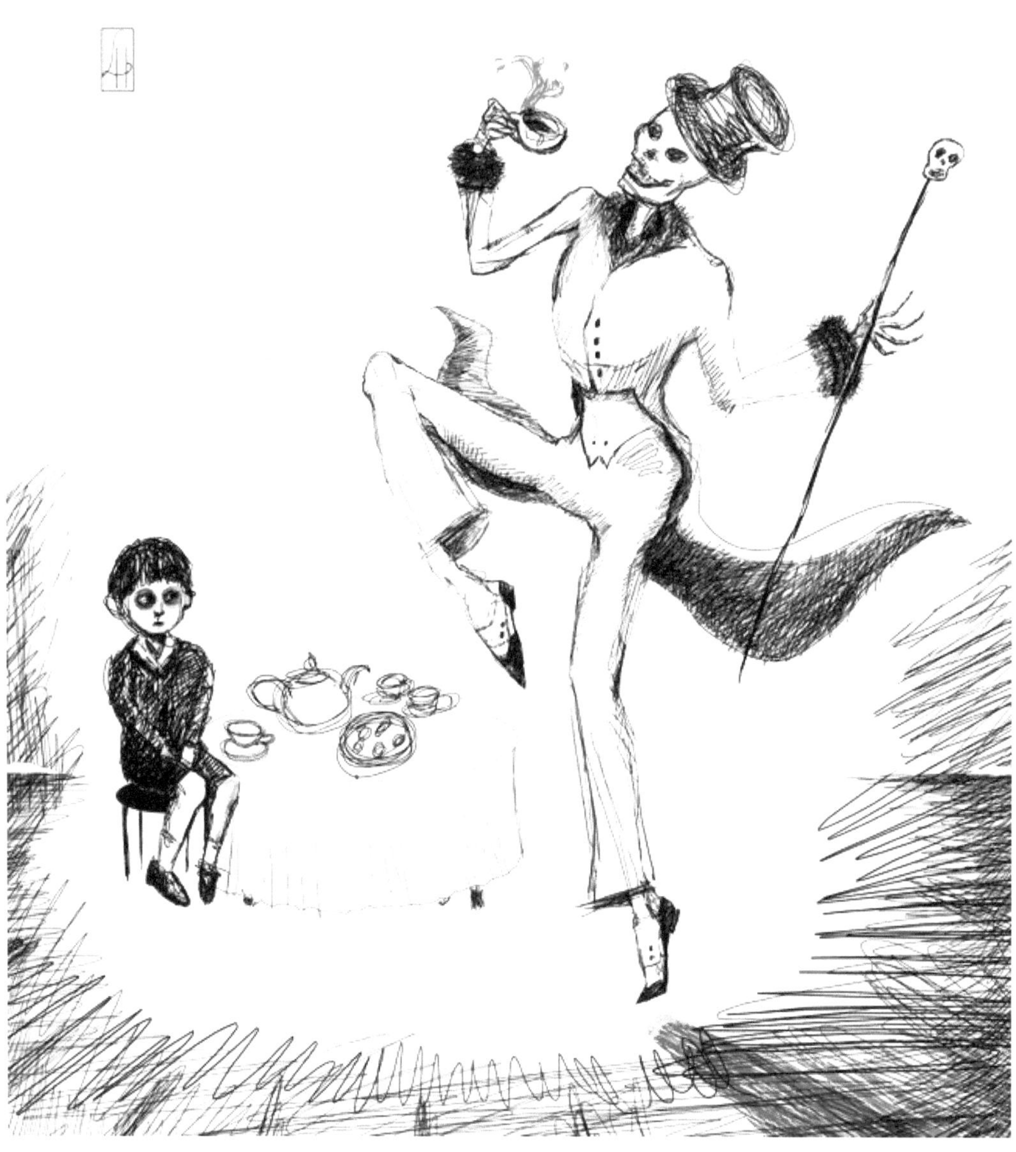

Mr. Death Meets Johnny, drawing by Leslie Hardie

For an Infant in the Throes of a Fatal Condition

Rob Hardin

Cirrhosis isn't half as bad
As maladies you might have had.
A failing liver strains the muscles
But liberates the red corpuscles.
When voided kidneys soak one's dollies,
Relief, like spasms, comes in volleys.
Rope-severed cords force coded silence,
Deterring tongues from false compliance.
Lung injuries from mustard gas
Loose sprinkles on Death's demitasse.
Torn ligaments beneath your bruises
Yield percs for opiated snoozes.
A scalpel, swallowed in mid-seizure,
Can point the way to lifelong leisure.
Wee hemophiliacs who stumble
Bring joy to cutthroats prone to fumble.
The tendency to swallow tacks
Inks spittle to a sputtered fax.
Cribs fraught with sanguine complication
Are catapults of grave elation.
Brief candle!, melting with distress,
You'll harden soon with seal's impress.

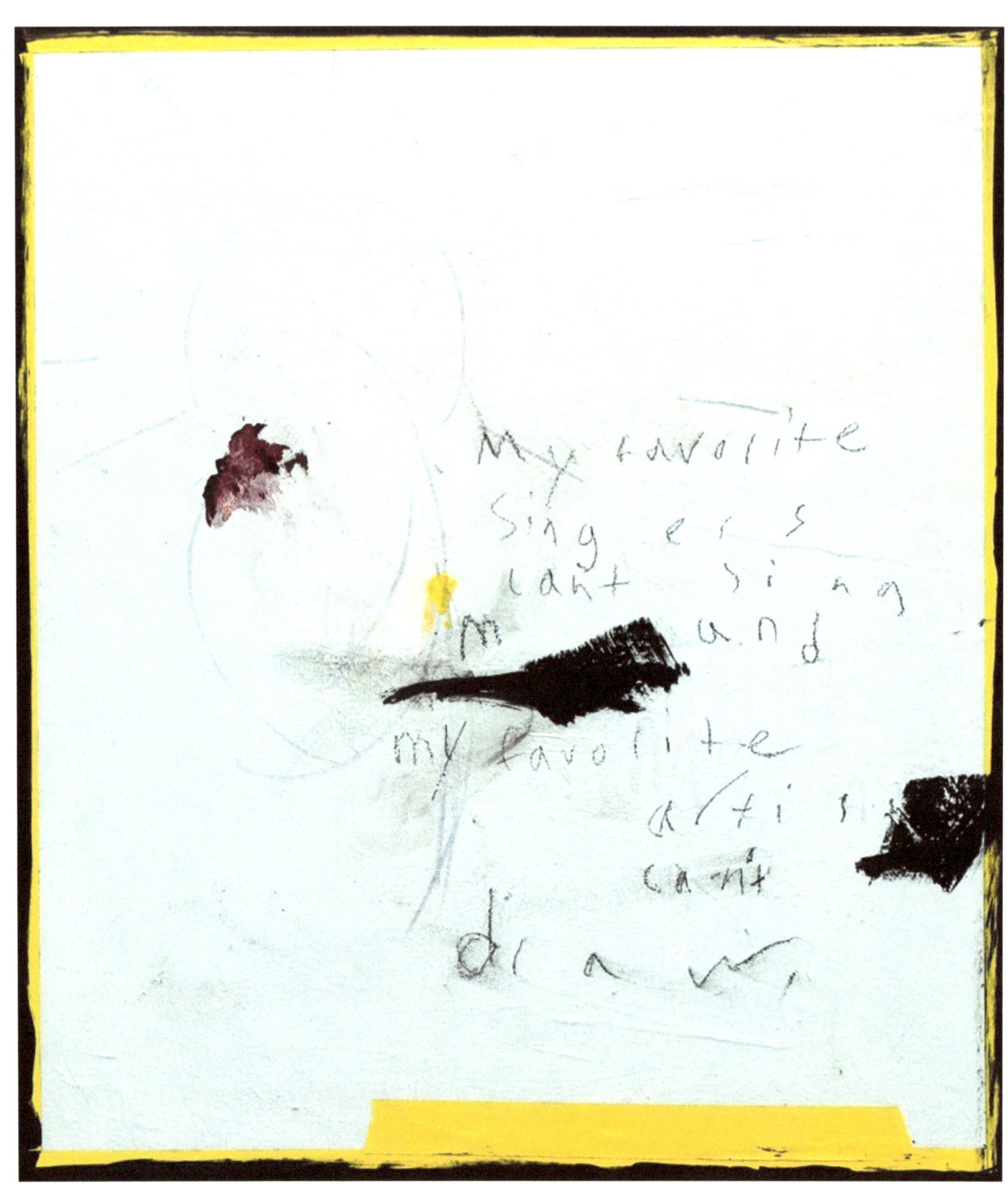

Singers can't sing, acrylic, oil stick, tape and gel medium on canvas, 30" x 22", 2010, by Joseph O'Neal

Landscape with a Bear in It Somewhere

Rebecca Weiner Tompkins

The limber late light
travels across the ridge
where the bear climbed.
Even with my head thrown back
I still can't take in the tops
of the tall pointed trees
up there. A friend's death
is flickering in and out
of my mind the whole time
I'm watching the yellow binding
weave slowly, lower and lower
down the slope of dusk-deepening
green and I expect the bear
to reverse his way,
track back down
to us, to give
a faster swipe of darkness
to the day's last lit edge
draining any hope I had
that this dying
would not happen
again.

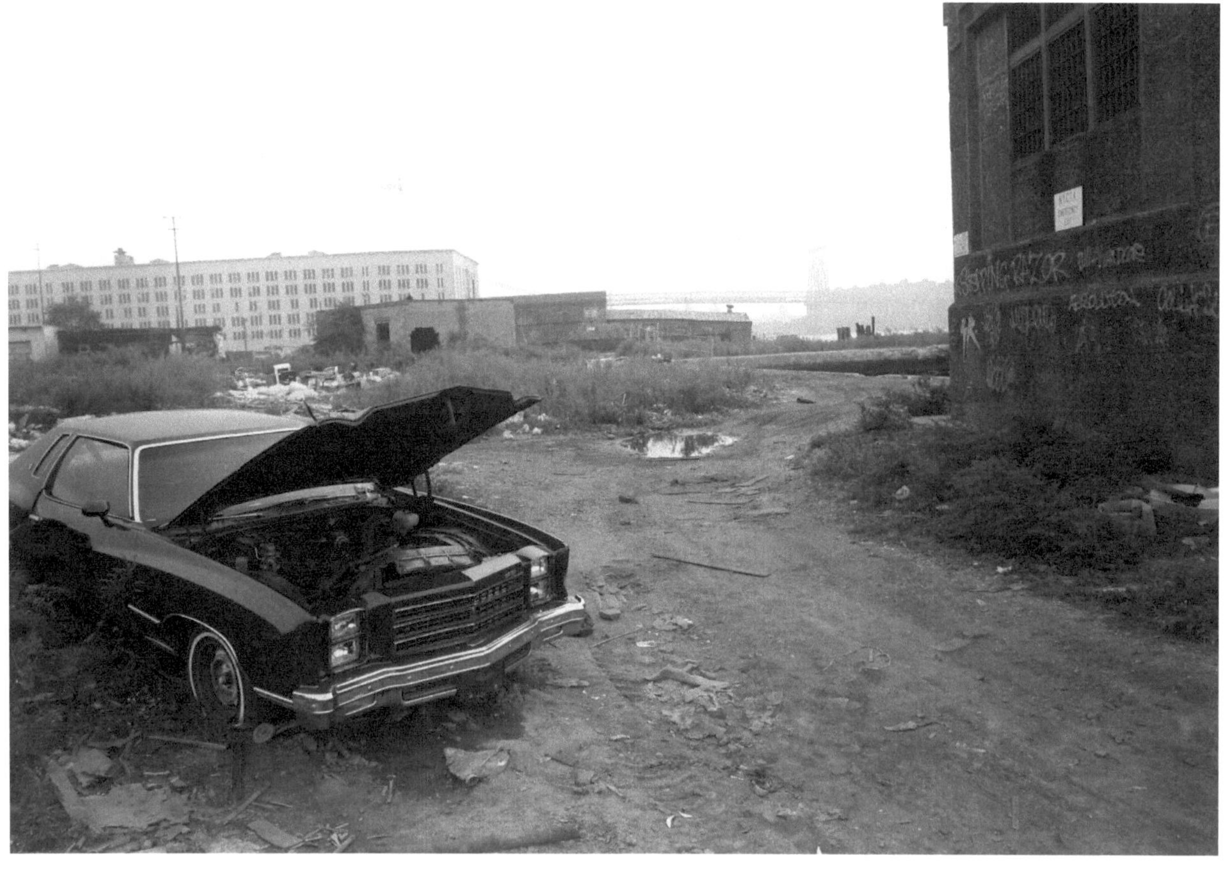

Photograph by Ted Barron

Last Supper in an Airport

Ron Richardson

Dawdle. Doodle. What to do?
Spill an alphabet, spill a stew.
Fire the cauldron, eat the bread,
soon those waiting will be dead.
Down the supper, drink the curse;
no matter how dull, death is worse.

Kiss of Kind

Carl Watson

Virtue and Fear
Stare at each other in the mirror,
They feed upon & tease each other
Until neither one remembers what it used to be.
That mirror's name is Vanity,
It can make a body live in harmony
With an improbable costume
Or it can make life hell,
A reflection of itself that is less than
Either extreme: divinity or banality.
Time does not, however,
Pander to faith's creation.
Thus if & when
God admires a loving-glass,
Be he drunk or vain,
It's said he sees the Devil there,
And when the Devil does the same
He enjoys a God.
In their conceit, each sees
Believes & acts the Other.
They are in spirit, each other,
They kiss, and two skulls
Wrapt in strained and stained habits
Of anthropoid flesh
Are thus made One.
As Judas was Jesus's need,
The dubious act he requisitioned, to be or not
The seed in history
From whence a world evolved to doubt; and
That such a question continues
Means, simply
It was never any different.
A most intimate lipskin
Seals this secret:
God betrayed the devil with a kiss because
He loved him,
If only as a notion.
And the sky cries with this searing, this long & loving
Adhesive smack!
Of apprehension, until at last—
A bridge of sighs.

And that fragile speed between enemies
Now seems forever tied on a tether of bliss
As lovers must forever part, their lips racing fast away
From that vaguest of cosmic decimal points:
Our defiant affection.

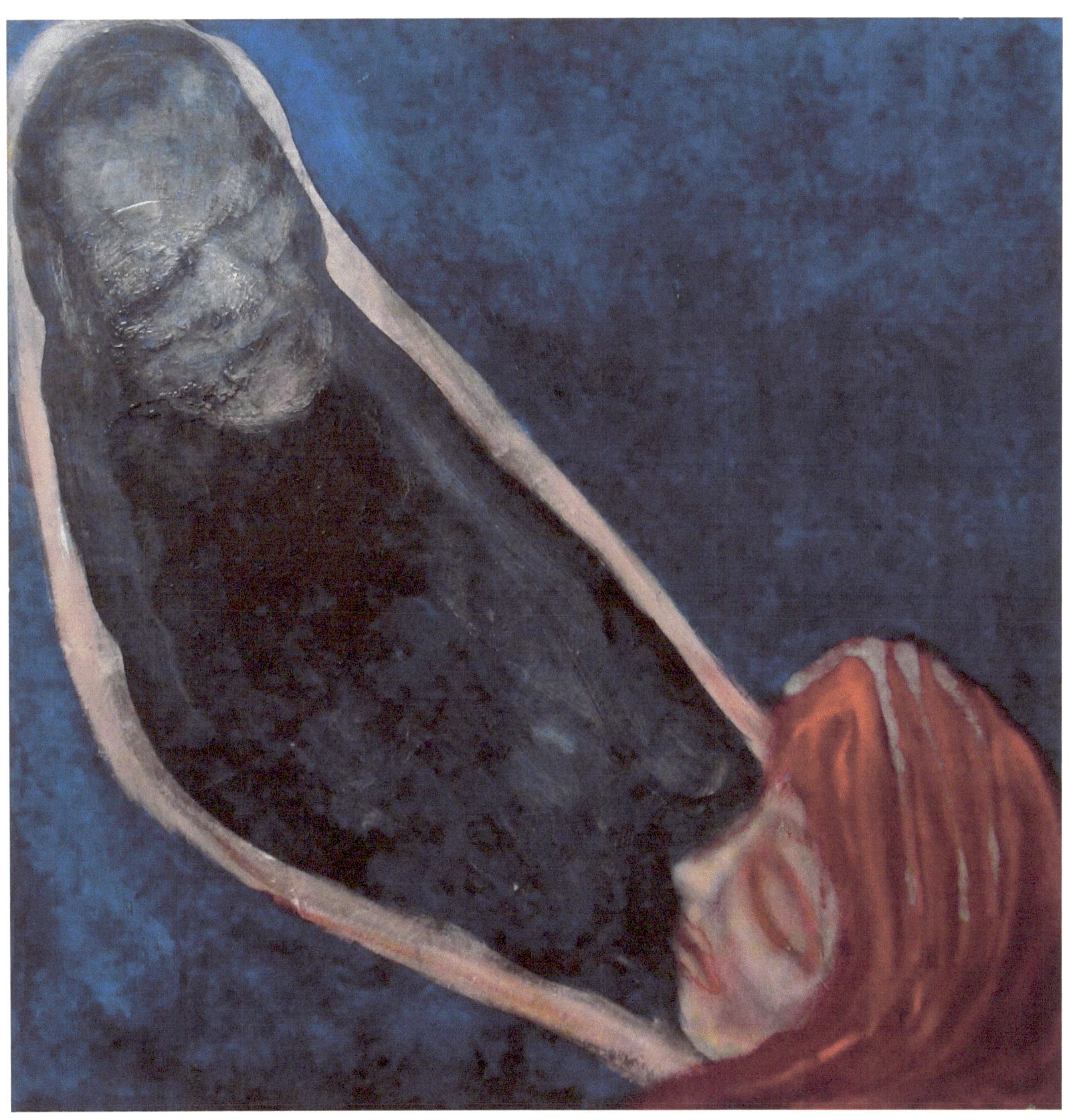

Untitled, oil on canvas, 36" x 36", 1998, by Charles Schick

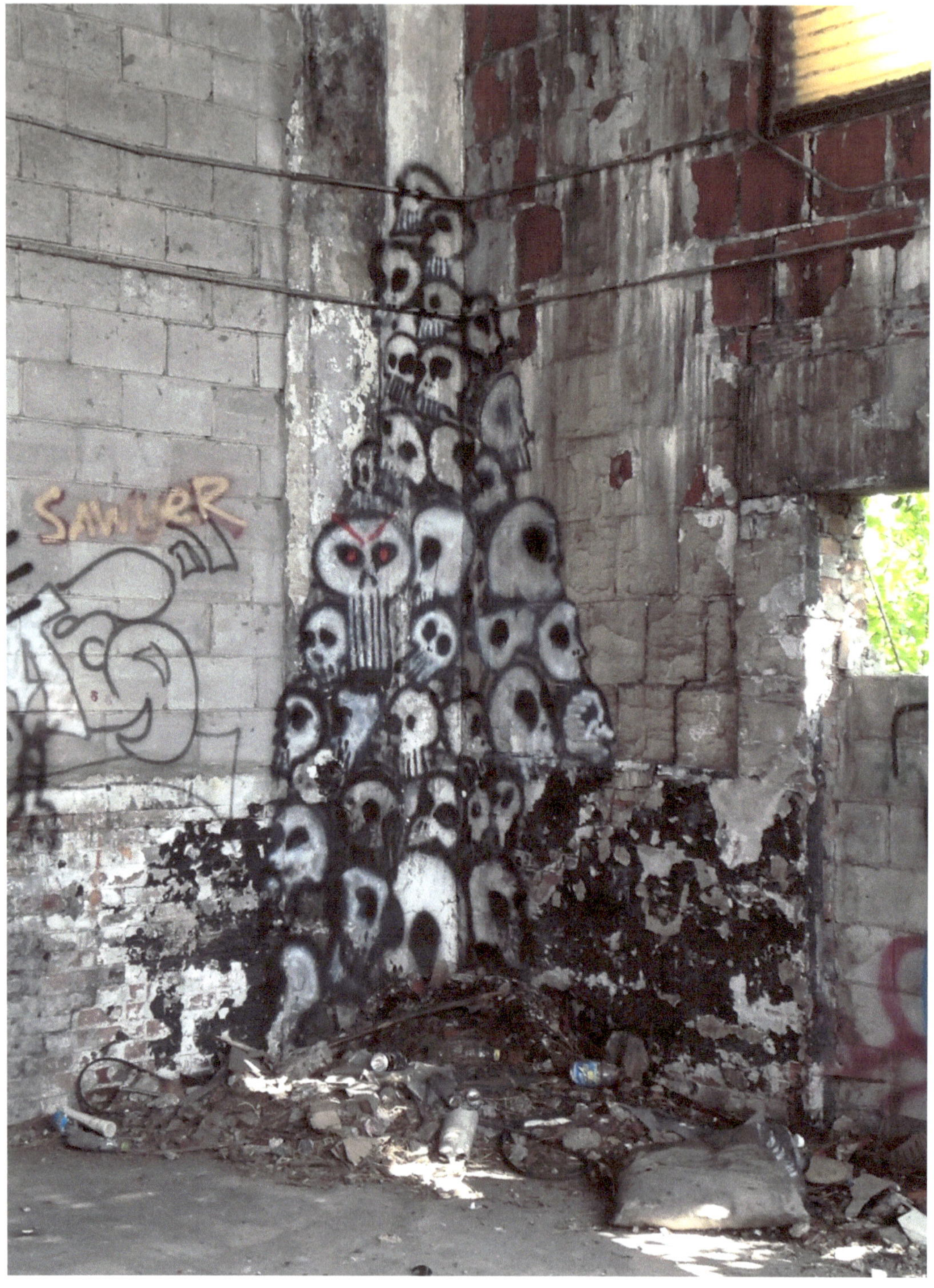

Photograph by Dennis Gordon

Call Up

John Farris

Today the world is wet & white: everybody tries
to throw the snow back (a girl, determined, handles a shovel
gingerly, sends a pile of it scattering; it flies

to the court below, exposing a red-stained Kreolite
stair, freeing it, contemplation of her handiwork, the novelty
of it in her face) to where the rain can dispatch it,

dispose of it (might have to call up the city,
might have to call up the sanitation department, might have
to call up the fire department, dig a deep pit

to throw it in), to run it off, to swell up the river
with it, the tide spinning sooty, frozen blocks down past
the Word Trade Center; out into the harbor!

The other day the sun was unusually warm; we
dared to walk in Prospect Park, to insepct the lily pond
in the botanical gardens: it was nice to see
the rhododendron bush in your backyard survived!

The Viewing

David Rattray

The wife spoke to me
by name:
"Thanks so much for coming,
David." Some didn't
want to see him. One
wouldn't even go in. I did.
I touched his hand.
It was as if he were only
sleeping, soft and warm.
I never felt one so
lifelike. They've
come a long way.
After a bit,
no one noticed,
I went back.
I touched him
on the hand again. It was
warm, and soft,
still. In August I
spent two weeks picking
blackberries on a New Hampshire
hill. Each berry
heavy and wet, the
size of a fat grape to be
checked for mold, then chucked
into a colander, an old
favorite of bright
yellow plastic, or if
too far gone, into the
tangle underfoot, under a
cloud of flies and
yellowjackets in the hot sun.
My skin all blood and
juice — fingers, wrists,
forearms streaming —
stained purple in a stench
as of a winepress.
A solo wasp
hovered over a sodden
cluster and at last lit down
on the rottenest

berry for a long sip,
then staggered out
over a sagging
leaf, to topple and buzz off
in a tight
Immelmann straight into the
inscrutable
mute raw incandescent
source of it all, only to
return over and over
to the reeking fruit
where in the end
it lay out flat in the
middle of a long red stain
like a naked Jonah
resting in his vine.
Just then there was a
spinning as of, let's say, an
autogyro
directly overhead,
and for a second there
it looked like Christ Himself
in the cockpit, bareheaded,
sporting green-tinted goggles
amid a nimbus of white flames
glimpsed through a dark
tunnel of vines and leaves
from where I scrambled
on my hands and knees
for cover in the deepest shade.
In the dream called
The Viewing the body's
still warm, as though
only asleep, maybe even
dreaming of being a
man watching a dead-drunk
wasp in a blackberry
patch on a hillside in
New England, unless
perhaps the actual
viewing was that of a passed-out

hornet dreaming it was a
man, indeed a holy man,
and the action
an audience granted by an ash-smeared
sage in the burning ghats
of the soul's bridal chamber in the
tremor of delight that is the
foreplay of annihilation;
there's a billion
starry nights out there.
Who's the bride?
How come she knows my name?

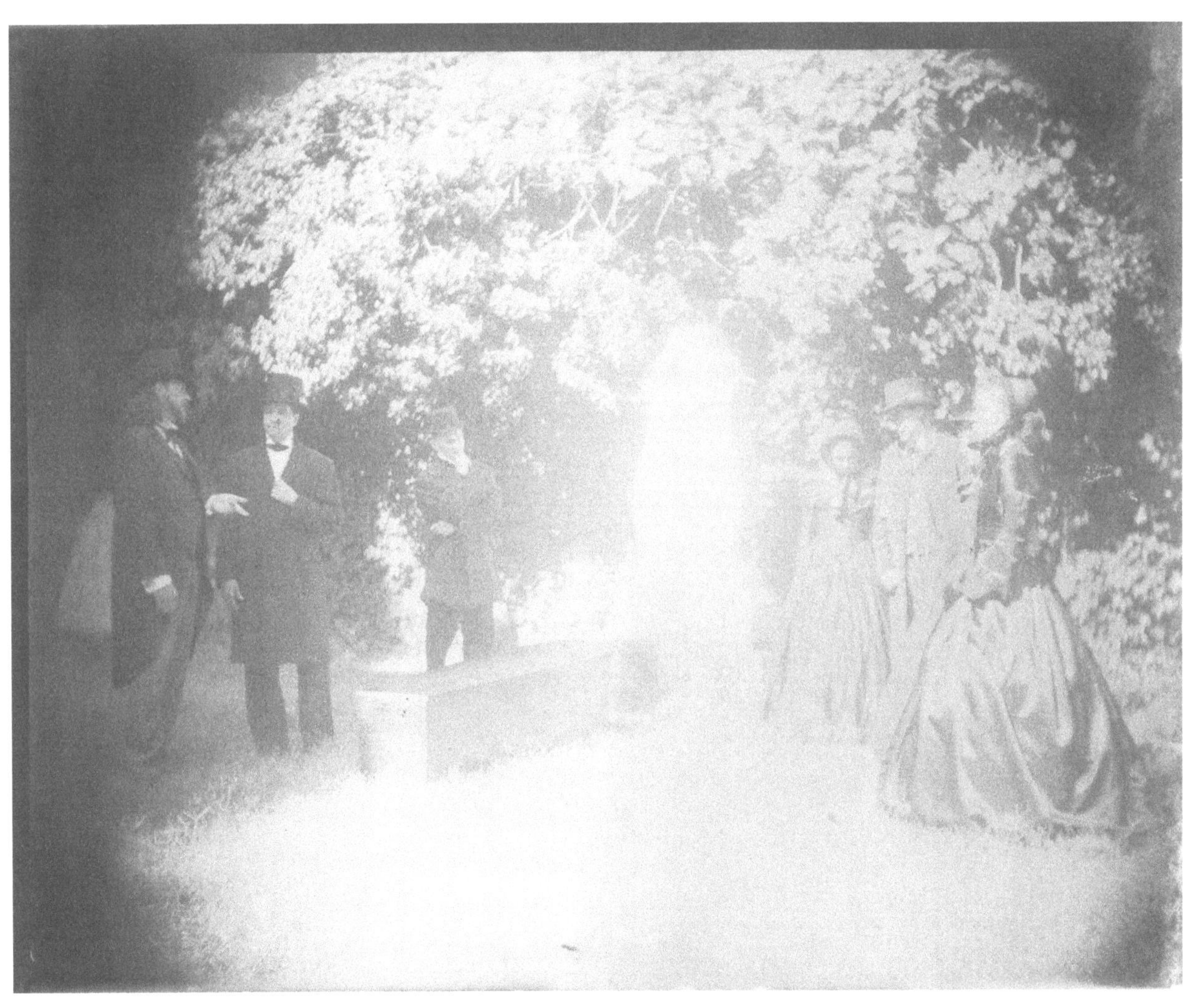

Photograph by Hal Hirshorn

off on grand boulevard

Norman Douglas

1.

fuck you fuck you fuck
you scribbled the self-
proclaimed, officially
acclaimed, pharmaceutically
addle-brained bourgeois
poet in morning electric's light.
okay, i added the burgher bit
because i'm talking city mouse
stalking across town & country
mouse, screaming at the wind
screen all that streaming text
one crazy-making dream.

2.

even now, i feel obla-dee-
blah-da-bligated to practice
tight restraints, indulge that
masochist with punishment,
discipline & sin n shit, n piss n
wesson oil, er, balsamic s-s-s-lime.
o joy!

3.

bumpity-bump groan the 4 wheels
under my ass dipped in empty pot-
holes, cracks, slipping, swerved pull-
in' the steer in, pushin' petals to their
mettle to a void, to cheat complete
catastrophe a victory for now. ow!
wow ow ow!
some words we have slurred into
utterly different sounds until utter
sounds like udder and motor rhymes
almost with murder, crash, bank!
the blood of a poet is only blood
transfused or tainted just like any other
professional amateur's sanguine
solutions, problems no better than ours,

words we all use like we cock them up,
toys to divert idled minds' details,
demons playing with twists rent
out of derisive howls keen to cut this
way, this perceptive palm over the eye,
a (ob)scene just, you're made to stand for rank, silent
truth.

detroit
january 2015

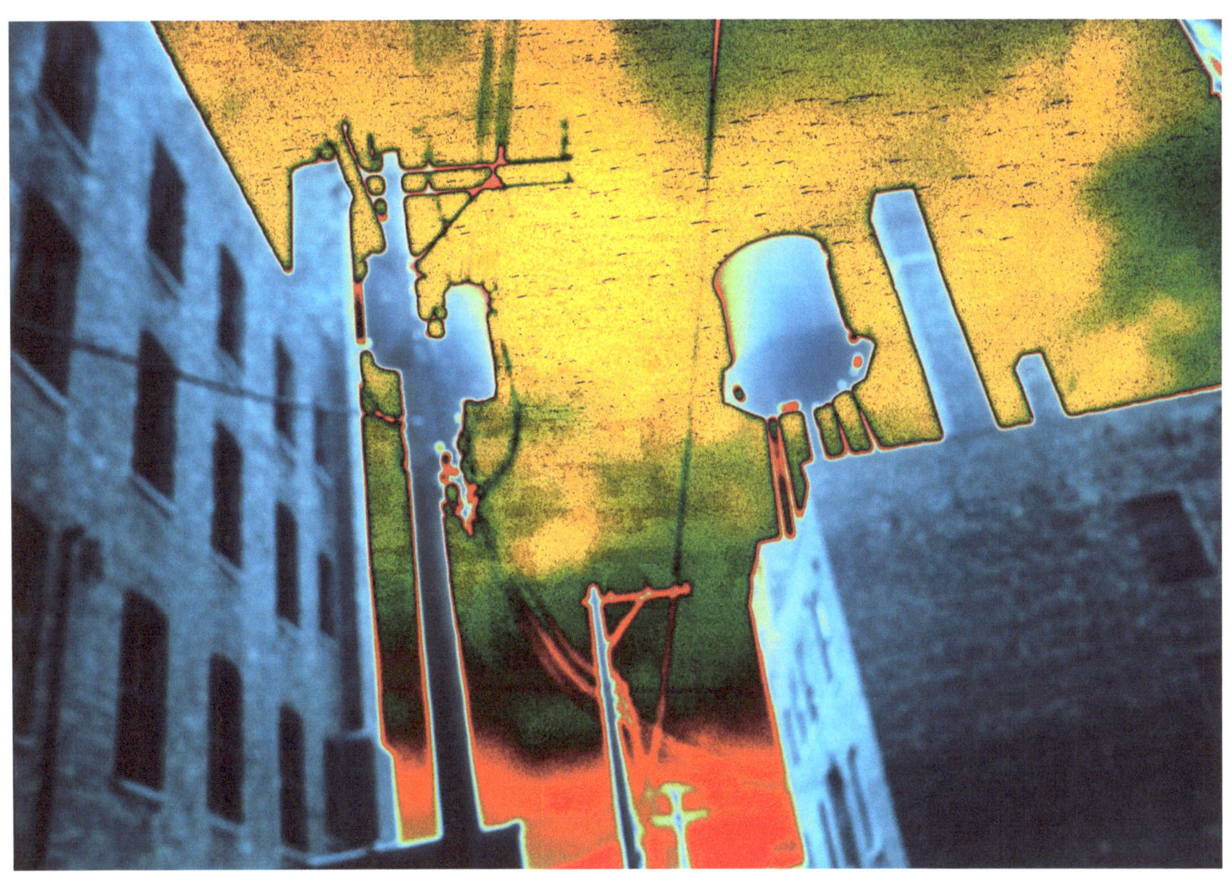

Photograph by Ruby Ray

I've Got My Shiny Kitten

Sharon Mesmer

—*for Yun Peng*

Hell yeah I'm skinny.
My body is COVERED in skin!
But I've got my shiny kitten
and I am not the same person I used to be.

Shopping naked with my shiny kitten
is like finding out that Beyoncé is experiencing
a powerful yearning to cram my gullet full of
Richard Nixon's head.
As you can plainly see,
I finally got my shiny new Frightened Cloned Care Bear
to dock with Skinny War Kitten.

And—ooh! Attention Deficit Trope!
I just got distracted by a toy machine, a cat,
the "melon-head" issue, another cat,
and a panda-cat named Rocket
who sings directly into an
alchemist's chest.
Do physical objects act as stand-ins
when informational things are hard to come by?
Probably.
But that's because shiny kitten's hairballs
keep calling my mom a hypocrite.

I've got my shiny kitten.
I've also got 18 shiny butcher knifes
18 silver shrimp forks
18 slime-covered linoleum swords
and 25 Yeti meat staves
Did any of that help me when I lost five close buddies
and half my ass
to my goddamn shiny kitten?
Nope.

Getting kneecapped by shiny kitten:
Boom! Coconut Effect! Fake Scottish Accent!
Winter is fluffy and white from solstice to equinox,
and so is shiny kitten
which makes this something of a Chunky Salsa Rule
in the context of a Zombie Apocalypse
caused by Kraut Osmosis.

Until I got kneecapped, I could read an entire library
in under 2 hours.
And that's why I'm now seriously considering
kneecapping shiny-ass kitten.
It's kitten hittin' time, yo.

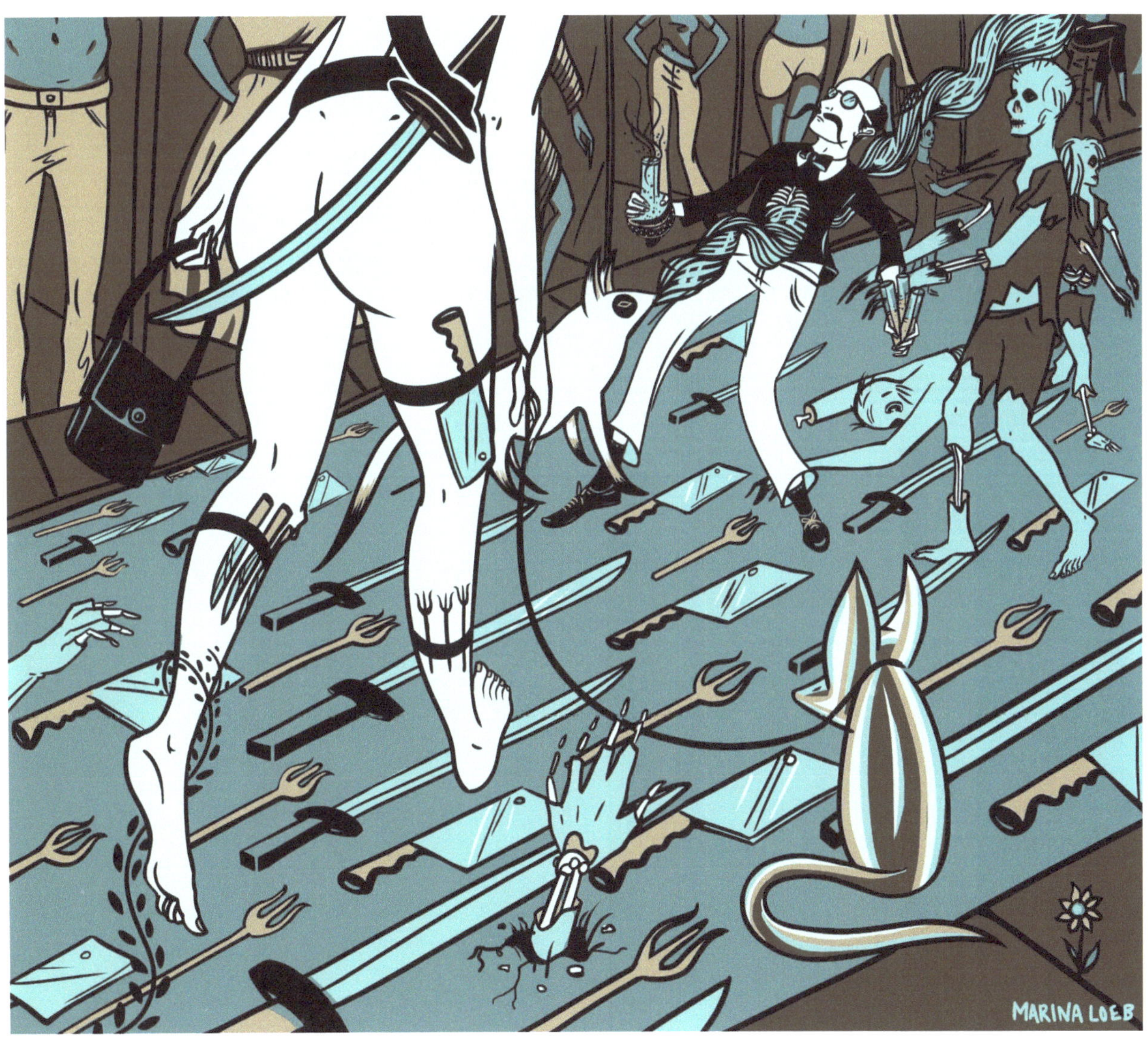

Illustration by Marina Loeb

Flack from Taylor

Taylor Mead

A President who makes war
Against and on Behalf of the
Worst of the Arab world.
Who sells the country to the
Japanese government and its subsidized
corporations.
Who is a mealy-mouthed lying bastard
Banker.
Who doesn't give a shit for his dog
except as a vote-getter.
Welcome to 1992—
Mayor Dinkins, who is a rubber stamp
Koch
Who is a bourgeois black
tennis player
That despises the Homeless, who closes
parks and removes benches, who
lets the police operate at their leisure
and only against the helpless.
Police who on Thanksgiving Day go after
sidewalk vendors.
Police who drive by car break-ins and muggings.
Who are never never there!
Who get pay raises while
others get booted from and
in their jobs.
A Mayor who wouldn't know how to
spend Federal money even if he had it . . .

TV stations that suck up to
the police—
that ignore the disastrous
consequences of the fall of the
Berlin Wall in order to praise Capitalism,
that ignore the riots all over
Europe—
That have discussions between
right-wing democrats and right
wing republicans and
call it equal time.

Oh I wrote a poem to a tree,
And the Mayor and the President
Came along and pissed on it,
And the tree died.

Does that leave a poem?

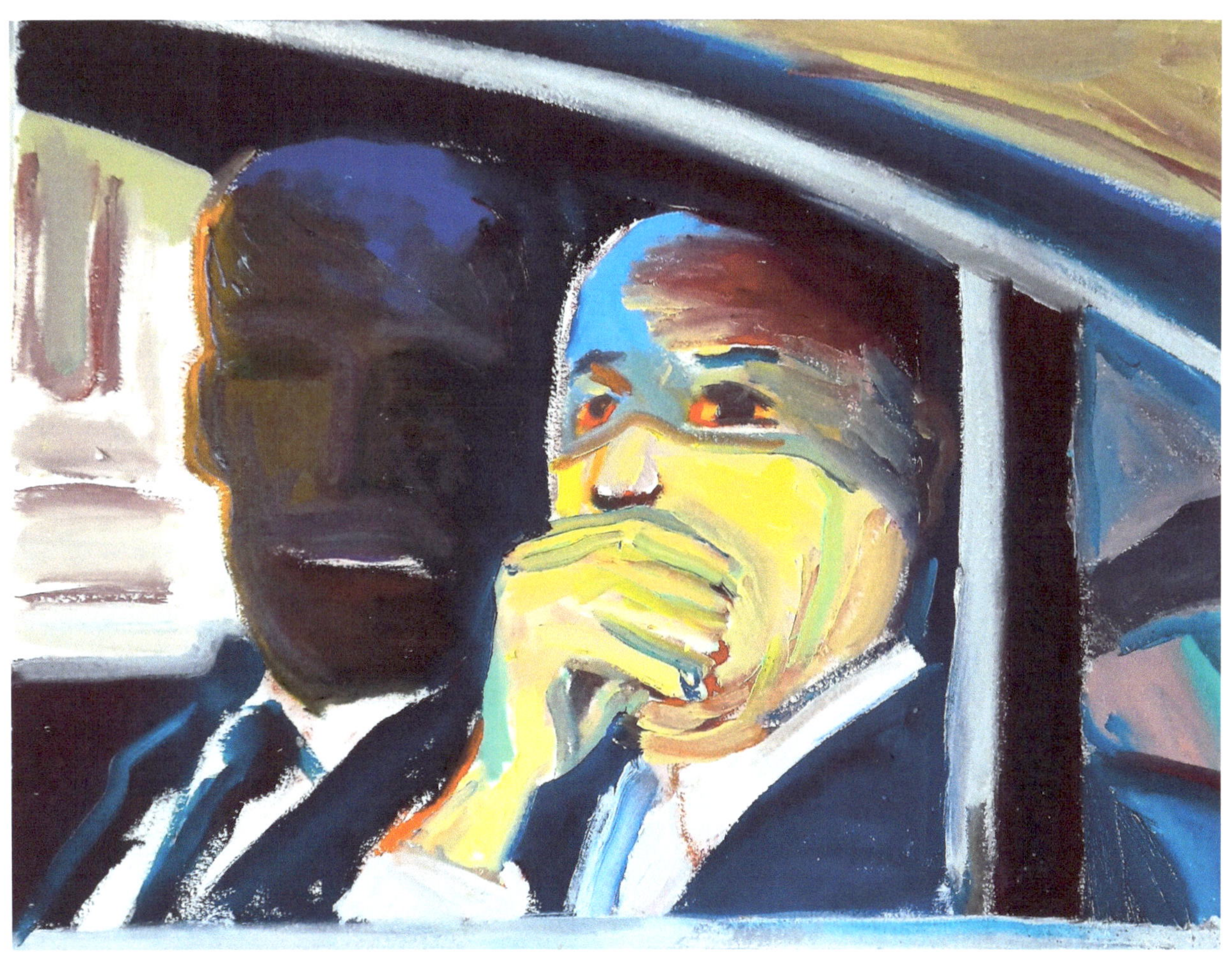

The Senator Gets the News the World Is Burning, oil on sized paper, 11" x 14", 2014, by Stephen Lack

Suspect Device

Michael Carter

In a cold stone cabin
In a deserted Cill Rialaig solstice-tide,
West wind wailing through drafty rafters,
Enounced aloud "Hrothgar Skyldinga"
& your Beowulf by turf-light,
Huddled in checkered blue Irish wool blankets:
Those dragons were real, and Grendel's
Avenging mom an otherworldly force

Today in my W.C. scriptorium,
See you pensive by the quay,
By the powerhouse, dog end
Squeezed between squat fingers;
Hyperbolically mirror its creamsicle twin stacks,
On a gray day in 1982—
About the time I first heard that clear voice,
At the Y, uptown with Bob Fitzgerald?
I think you'd just set *Sweeney Astray,*
Were yet for Station Island, all
These meanderings of soul into light

White-haired wizen of the boglands,
Of bog queens and gold hoards,
Sing of the human condition, of the rocks in it,
& dig, dig-it man, deeper layers, below
The peat through crust to the very mantle—
You took the mantle and held it
Far more years on an island strewn with wordsmiths,
I had luck to apprentice,

To learn to hear
The ancient sounds of stones your ear
Attuned one to . . . . Lucky to meet twice more:
Reviving broke days of old Mexico with Phil Kelly,
Bespoke exuberant color, glowing citadels,
Lush hills, en la casita del ambasador,
On a cold Raglan Road,
With a glass of red wine and shot of Patron
Or four

Words were your religion; Bloody Ulster, all the North
A virtual garrison then, farmers and peat diggers

Scrutinized as any intellectual;
Made the case for measure
With unerring aim,
Poetry a suspect device for damn sure

Or near the end, your birthday
Stealing tight sips from the Jameson-jar.
As a global horde of translators try hard
Not to murder your voice with local idiom,
In the time-hallowed Trinity pews
(Not a hundred yards from the Bolus vitrine),
And you wouldn't sign no more books;
Jaysus, Mary and Joseph, no more
Would your celebrity create instant commodities,
For tourist poetasters

All the instruments agree,
The day of his death musta been a hot one,
(At least by Irish standards),
But no bombs set off in commemoration,
Except within the inner ear, for
Your voice and Voyager
Hit interstellar space about the same time

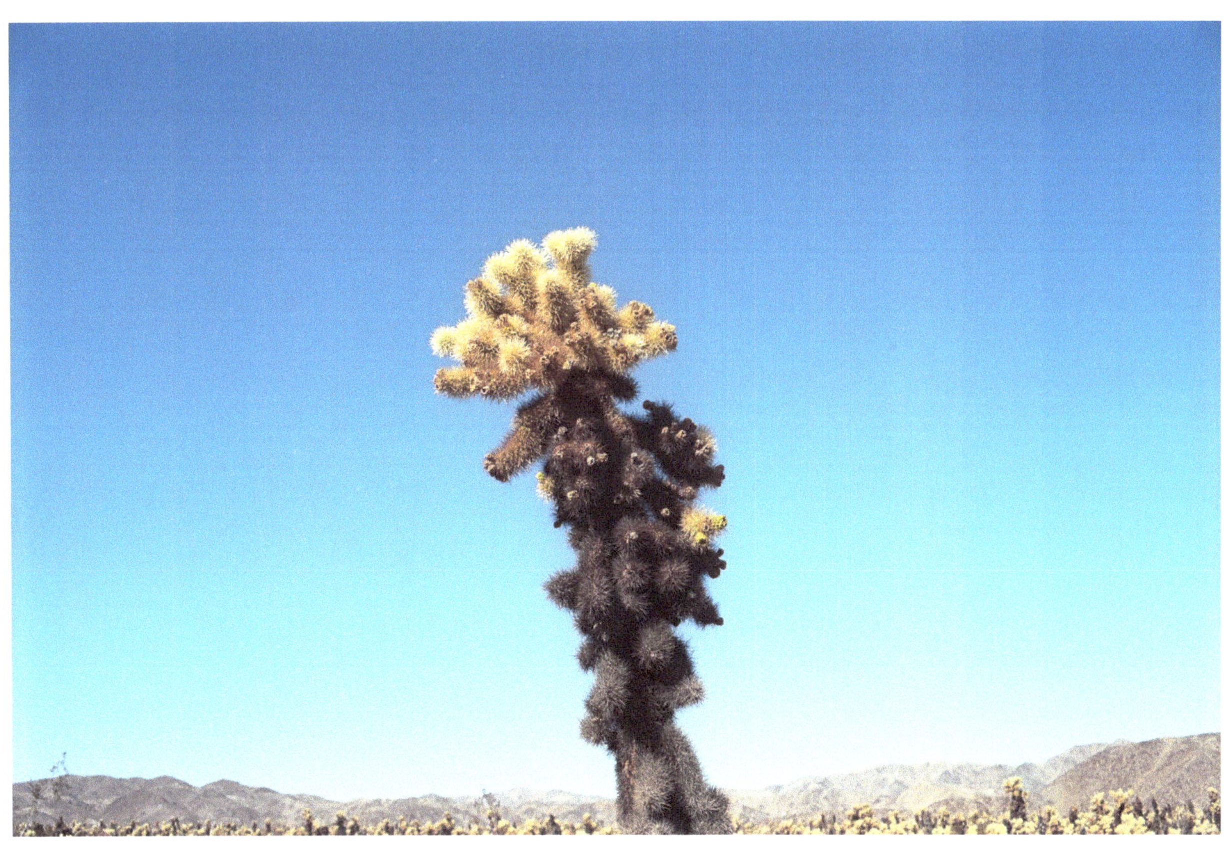

Photograph by Justin Clifford Rhody

You

Vladimir Mayakovsky

Ты
Пришла—
деловито,
за рыком,
за ростом,
взглянув,
разглядела просто мальчика.
Взяла,
отобрала сердце
и просто
пошла играть—
как девочка мячиком.
И каждая—
чудо будто видится—
где дама вкопалась,
а где девица.
«Такого любить?
Да этакий ринется!
Должно, укротительница.
Должно, из зверинца!»
А я ликую.
Нет его—
ига!
От радости себя не помня,
скакал,
индейцем свадебным прыгал,
так было весело,
было легко мне.

You
Walked up—
businesslike,
because of my roar,
because of my height,
took one look,
and saw I was just a boy.
Without a second thought,
you took my heart away
and simply
went off to play—
like a girl with a ball.
And every woman,
as if witnessing a miracle,
is rooted to the ground—
over here, a lady; over there, a girl.
"Love someone like that?
That kind will pounce on you!
She must be a lion tamer.
She must be from the zoo!"
But I was rejoicing.
It's gone—
that burden!
Out of my mind with joy,
I was jumping,
I was leaping like an Indian at a wedding,
that's how happy I felt,
how light.

translation by Jenny Wade

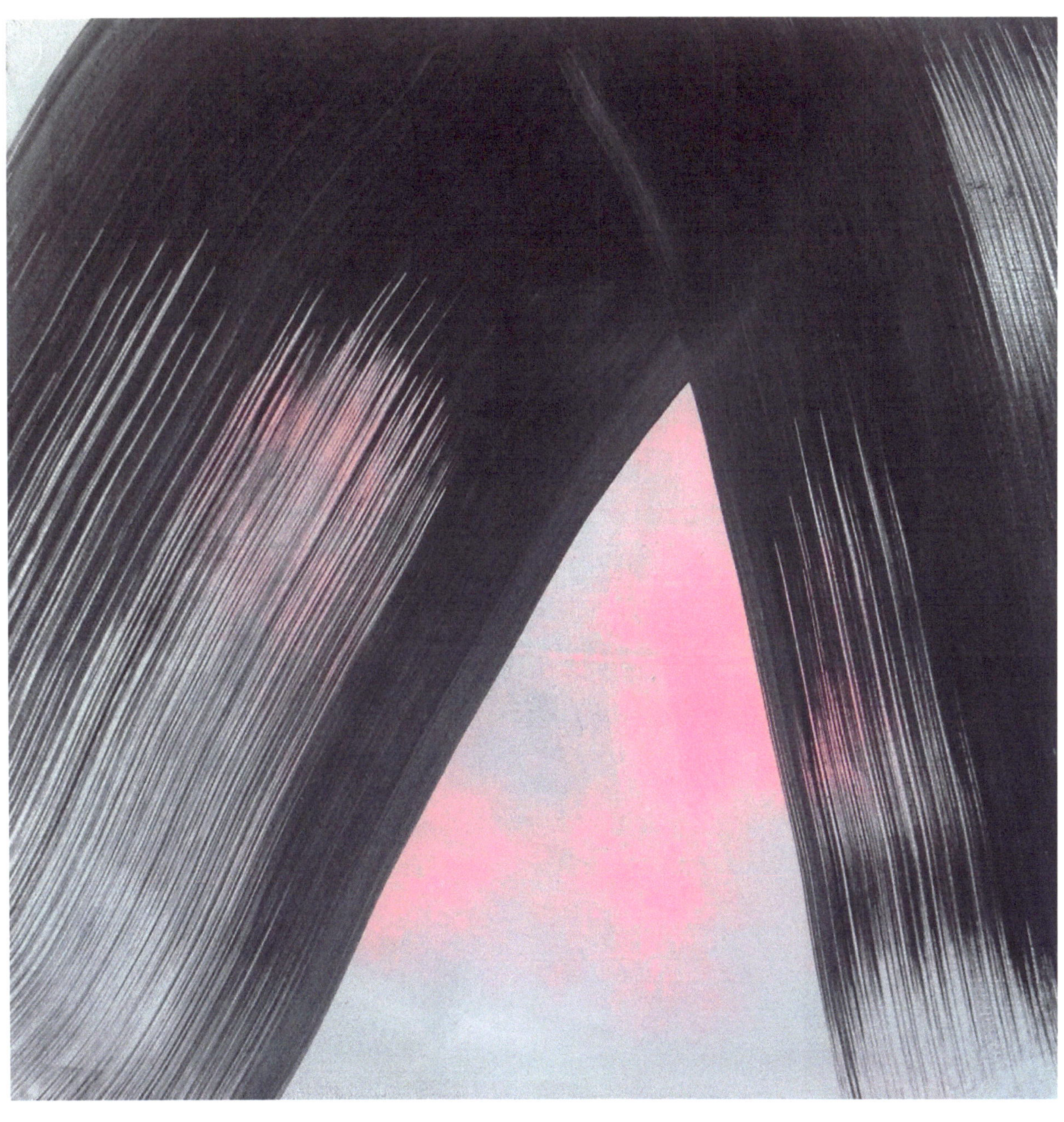

Lambent 42, oil and spray paint on linen, Justine Frischmann

The Doctor, Part 97

Sean Flaherty

The way my fingers fit
beginning at the sternum,
moving along
the rib bones,

each time I see
the Doctor,
each time I leave her office
it seems
easier
to say
"I am dying."

I asked again
to grab reality by the tail,
"what if I stop taking
all this medicine,
what if I
stop
doing
all this stuff
that makes me hurt,
that makes me
always
uncomfortable?"

she says she's not sure
but
the studies show
a life expectancy of
six months
without treatment,

I reach
for
the bones in my back
when I scratch them
when I ask
feel like seashells
like an ancient trigger
to
let the water
pour out my eyes,
to
let myself hear it:

"I am dying."

17 December 2014

Sean Flaherty, November 15, 1966–January 4, 2015

Photograph by Jeff Spirer

Contributors

David Rattray was a poet, translator and scholar, who was fluent in most Western languages, as well as Sanskrit, Latin, and Greek. Published by City Lights Books in 1963, Rattray's Artaud translations were some of the first and best in English. His book, *How I Became One of the Invisible*, was published by Semiotext(e) shortly before his untimely death in 1992.

Taylor Mead (December 31, 1924 – May 8, 2013) was an American writer, actor and performer. Mead, "the first underground movie star," according to J. Hoberman of *The Village Voice*, appeared in several of Andy Warhol's underground films, including *Tarzan and Jane Regained... Sort of* (1963) and *Taylor Mead's Ass* (1964). He had roles in many films; his final appearance was in Jim Jarmusch's 2003 *Coffee and Cigarettes*. He was the author of numerous books of poetry, including *Taylor Mead on Amphetamine and in Europe* (Boss Books, 1968) and, most recently, *A Simple Country Girl* (Bowery Books, 2005).

Jack Micheline, born Harold Martin Silver, took his pen name from writer Jack London and his mother's maiden name. He moved to Greenwich Village in the 1950s, where he lived on the fringe of poverty, writing about hookers, drug addicts, blue collar workers, and the dispossessed. In 1957, Troubadour Press published his first book, *River of Red Wine*. Jack Kerouac wrote the introduction, and it was reviewed by Dorothy Parker in *Esquire* magazine. Micheline relocated to San Francisco in the early 1960s, where he spent the rest of his life. He published over twenty books, some of them mimeographs and chapbooks. Though he was one of the original Beats, Micheline characterized the Beat movement as a product of media hustle, and hated the label. He died of a heart attack while riding a BART subway train from San Francisco to Orinda in 1998.

Bob Holman was described by Henry Louis Gates Jr. in *The New Yorker* as "the postmodern promoter who has done more to bring poetry to cafes and bars than anyone since Ferlinghetti." He is a poet, multimedia producer, poetry activist and performance poetry professor who lives in New York City. Bob has published six books, most recently *A Couple of Ways of Doing Something* (Aperture, 2006), praise poems paired with photographs of artists by Chuck Close and *Sing This One Back to Me* (2013). He's put poetry on television, radio and the Web, producing *The United States of Poetry* for PBS, appearing on MTV's *Spoken Word Unplugged* and HBO's *Def Poetry Jam*, and serving as poetry commentator on WNYC and NPR. Currently, he teaches "Exploding Text: Poetry in Performance" at Columbia University and is the founder and proprietor of the Bowery Poetry Club.

Hal Sirowitz was a member of the 1993 Nuyorican Poetry Slam team and competed in the 1993 National Poetry Slam. Sirowitz has appeared on television programs such as MTV's *Spoken Word: Unplugged* and PBS's *The United States of Poetry*. He has written six books on poetry, including *Mother Said, My Therapist Said* and *Father Said*. Sirowitz is a 1994 recipient of an NEA Fellowship in Poetry and is the former Poet Laureate of Queens, New York. He worked as a special education teacher in the New York public school system for 23 years. He is married to the writer Mary Minter Krotzer.

Bonny Finberg has published fiction, personal essays, poetry, photographs and reviews. Her collection of short stories *How the Discovery of Sugar Produced the Romantic Era* was published by Sisyphus Press in 2006 and was documented in the feature-length video *5 Guys Read Finberg*. Publishers' Weekly said of her work in *Best American Erotica of 1996* (Simon & Schuster) that it "exudes a stunning sensual sensibility." Her work has been translated into French, Hungarian and Japanese. She has been included in the *Outlaw Bible of American Poetry* (Thunder's Mouth Press), as well as the anthologies *Unbearables, Crimes of the Beats, Help Yourself, The Worst Book I Ever Read.* (Autonomedia), and *Lost and Found: Stories from Mr. Beller's Neighborhood.* Also, the Love issue of *Van Gogh's Ear* and *Upstairs At Duroc*, both published in Paris. She is a contributor to *A Gathering of the Tribes* and *Le Purple Journal.* Her work has been aired on the radio in London and Amsterdam. She lives in Paris and New York.

Charles Gatewood's Wall Street work won two fellowships from the NY State Arts Council and the book was awarded the Leica Medal of Excellence for Outstanding Humanistic Photojournalism. Gatewood's other subjects include rock musicians, body art, artistic nudes, and portraits of underground icons he calls "obscure celebrities." Go to www.charlesgatewood.com for more info.

Stephen Lack has been painting and exhibiting internationally for over forty years. A seminal artist from the East Village Scene of the 1980s, he creates work that runs the gamut from political and interpersonal dramas to seemingly benign landscapes of America's greatest era. The subject of an *Arts and Minds* profile for Bravo TV, he recently held a retrospective of his car-related paintings, "Autonation," at the Illinois State School of the Arts in Normal, Illinois. Stephen has also participated in the making of several feature films, most notably *The Rubber Gun*, with Allan Moyle; *Scanners*, with David Cronenberg; and *All the Vermeers*, with Jon Jost. His paintings are in many American and international collections.

Sparrow lives in a doublewide trailer in Phoenicia, NY with his loyal wife Violet Snow. He is teaching himself to play atonal harmonica.

Peter Shear was born in 1980 in Beverly Farms, MA and currently lives in Bloomington, IN. His first solo exhibition, "Sausage," took place in May 2013 at the Peoria Art Guild, Peoria, IL; a second, "Dragon Express," was held in 2013 at Welcome Screen, London, UK. 2013 group exhibitions include "What I Like About You," organized by Julie Torres, Parallel Art Space, Brooklyn; and "Transposed Planes," with Seth Adelsberger and Stacy Fisher, LVL3, Chicago, IL. His work has received notice in the *Chicago Tribune, New City, Huffington Post, Knight Arts, Two Coats of Paint, Studio Critical* and the podcast *Studio Break.* A selection of his paintings is featured in *New American Paintings* #107.

Ron Richardson is a tangled mass of stories. He's a thumb-sucker, a brother, a playmate, a middle child, a dreamer, a tattletale, a friend, a saint, a nerd, a writer, a Taurus, a rebel, a hippie, a joker, a teacher, a boyfriend, a ghoul. He has taught English as a Second Language in Korea, Spain, Japan, and San Francisco and now teaches composition at City College of San Francisco and San Francisco State University. Find out more about his new book, *Narrative Madness*, at ronosaurusrex.com.

Dennis Gordon is a photographer and model creator whose primary subject is abandoned structures, particularly post-operative industrial buildings. Born in 1957 in New York, Gordon completed high school and embarked on a 36-year career with the FDNY in 1978. Through the '80s and '90s, Gordon resided in the Lower East Side, while undertaking stints as a performance artist and actor, while deepening his exploration of abandoned industrial sites across the U.S. His unique background as a highly decorated firefighter, visual artist and Buddhist elicited an invitation in 2014 to lecture at the Rubin Museum of Art. His current modeling project is a 1/87th scale reconstruction of post-apocalyptic America inspired by his early years in firefighting with the FDNY and life in the Lower East Side. He was featured in the Steve Buscemi documentary, *A Good Job: Stories of the FDNY.*

Natalia Evelyn Bencicova is a 21-year-old visual artist exploring mixed media and photography. She grew up in Bratislava, Slovakia and currently lives in Berlin. She began taking digital photographs two years ago and is trying to discover the point at which the commercial and the artistic meet.

Gretchen Faust is an artist and performer. She's had multiple solo exhibitions at the Pat Hearn Gallery in NYC and Greengrassi in London, where she is currently represented. She has performed at the Franklin Furnace and the Jack Tilton Gallery in NYC. She wrote regularly for *Art Forum* in the 1980s and 1990s, and now resides in Totnes, England.

Rebecca Weiner Tompkins has played and recorded acoustic and amplified four and five-string violin and viola with Karen and the Sorrows, Life in a Blender, Chief, Scott McClatchy, Patti Smith and many others. Her poems have appeared in various journals including *Poetry magazine, The Seneca Review, The Antioch Review, Ploughshares, Pequod,* and *The Mercury Reader*. In 2009 she gave a TED talk in Canterbury, Kent UK, "Sensing Convergences," which is also the title of a manuscript she's writing. After 25 years in the East Village, NYC she crossed the river to live near Prospect Park in Brooklyn, where she spends a lot of time wandering about with her dogs.

Sharon Mesmer's most recent poetry collections are *Annoying Diabetic Bitch* (Combo Books 2008) and *The Virgin Formica* (Hanging Loose 2008). Her two short fiction collections, *The Empty Quarter* and *In Ordinary Time* (Hanging Loose 2000 and 2005) were published together in French translation by Hachette Litteratures as *Ma Vie a Yonago* (trans., Daniel Bismuth) in 2005. A selection of her flarf poems appears in the just-released *Postmodern American Poetry: A Norton Anthology*. With other members of the flarf collective she read her work at the Whitney Museum, the Kelly Writers House at UPenn, and the Walker Arts Center in Minneapolis. Her essay on the life and death of flarf can be found at: www.wired.com/beyond_the_beyond/2013/08/ten-years-of-flarf-poetry/. She teaches at NYU, the New School and online for the Chicago School of Poetics, and has received awards from the Fulbright Commission, the New York Foundation for the Arts and the Jerome Foundation (as mentor to grantee Elisabeth Workman).

Michael Randall is a writer, musician, filmmaker and visual artist who lives in New York City. His work has appeared in numerous literary magazines and anthologies. More can be found at www.michaelrandallnyc.com.

Ron Kolm is one of the founding members of the Unbearables literary collective, and an editor of several of their anthologies: *Crimes of the Beats, The Worst Book I Ever Read* and *The Unbearables Big Book* *of Sex!* Ron is an associate editor of the *Evergreen Review*. He is the author of *The Plastic Factory* and the co-author, with Jim Feast, of the novel, *Neo Phobe*. A collection of his poems, *Divine Comedy*, has just been published by Fly By Night Press. He's had work published in *Live Mag!*, *Gathering of the Tribes* and *The Outlaw Bible of American Poetry*. Kolm's papers were purchased by the New York University library, where they've been catalogued in the Fales Collection as part of the Downtown Writers Group.

Steve Dalachinsky's work has appeared in journals on and off line, including *Big Bridge, Milk, Unlikely Stories, Xpressed, Ratapallax, Evergreen Review, Long Shot, Alpha Beat Soup, Xtant, Blue Beat Jacket, N.Y. Arts Magazine, 88* and *Lost and Found Times*. He is included in such anthologies as *Beat Indeed; The Haiku Moment; Up Is Up But So Is Down: New York's Downtown Literary Scene, 1974-1992* and *The Outlaw Bible of American Poetry*. Dalachinsky is the author of many books. Among his recent ones are *A Superintendent's Eyes* and *Fool's Gold*. Steve also writes a monthly column about music, "Outtakes," for *The Brooklyn Rail*.

Marc Olmsted's work has appeared in *City Lights Journal, New Directions in Prose & Poetry, The Outlaw Bible of American Poetry, Signs of Life, Processed World, Bongo Chalice, Blue Satellite* and a variety of small press publications. About him, Allen Ginsberg said this: "Marc Olmsted inherited Burroughs' scientific nerve & Kerouac's movie-minded line nailed down with gold eyebeam in San Francisco." His work includes two books, *Milky Desire* and *Résumé*.

Pete Simonelli grew up in Stockton, CA, spent nearly 20 years in San Francisco, many of them playing in bands, writing poems and tending bar at Doc's Clock and around the Mission. His published works include *Night Sees You First* (AJBK Press, 2005), *A Lonely War* (Lancashire and Somerset, 2008), and *One Brittle Nerve* (Lancashire and Somerset, 2010). His band Enablers has recorded five CDs and toured extensively, here and in Europe. Pete moved to Brooklyn in 2007, where he is co-curator of the peerless performance series Picasso Machinery.

Carl Watson is a writer living in NYC. He has published some books, including *Beneath the Empire of the Birds* (short stories) by Apathy Press, and *The Hotel of Irrevocable Acts* (a novel) by Autonomedia. These books have also been published in France, by Vagabonde Press and Gallimard, respectively. Recently Vagabonde has published *Une Vie Psychosomatique*. His latest novel, *Backwards the Drowned Go Dreaming*, was published by **SENSITIVE SKIN BOOKS** in 2012. Watson also writes regular opinionated essays (under several names) for the *Williamsburg Observer*, an anarchist publication that originated at the Right Bank Cafe in Brooklyn. Currently he is working on a book about Henry Darger's autobiography, which he hopes will dispel the myth of literature and romantic genius and condemn all writers to the category of biological machines engaged in redundant self-constitution no different from the growth of crystals, the birth of stars, or the splitting of amoeba. Watson drinks to get through his day.

Max Blagg was born in England and has lived in New York City since 1971. He is the author of four collections of poetry, as well as other books. His most recent publication *The Little Dress Book* (Shallow Books), was listed in *About Poetry's* top twenty small press publications of 2010. He has collaborated with various artists, including Alex Katz, Jack Pierson, Richard Prince and Keith Sonnier. With Glenn O'Brien, Blagg coedited the legendary art/lit/tit magazine, *Bald Ego*. He is a contributing editor to *Oyster, BG* and *10 Magazine,* and is on the faculty at the School of Visual Arts. His "embellished memoir," *Ticket Out,* was published in 2013, and a new collection of poems, *Slow Dazzle,* is forthcoming.

Sean Flaherty wrote poems about Brooklyn and commuting on the subway since 1989. He has self-published works such as *Cannibal Love: No Regrets* (1991) and *Skinny White Beer Machine* (1994) by having multiple artists bind the books which were then included in shows at locations such as Kelly Lamb's Thicket Gallery and the National Arts Club. His work has appeared on *Green Spot Blue* once a week since December 2010. Currently *Green Spot Blue* is running all 55 of his subway pomes, once a week, including a brief introduction to the series at *www.greenspotblue.com/world/2011/5/18/a-brief-introduction-to-subway-pomes.html.* You can read the complete Doctor Series of poems, chronicling his battle with cancer, at *https://medium.com/@seanflaherty/the-doctor-series-94db34a12d3d.* He passed away on January 4, 2015.

David West is an American artist who lives in Paris. He's lived in New York for long stretches of time, as well as in San Francisco and Chicago.

Justine Frischmann is an artist and musician who has performed and exhibited in Europe, North America, Japan and Australia. She wrote and performed with Elastica and, more recently, has written for and produced a number of artists including M.I.A. She has a degree in architecture from University College London, has studied Contemplative Art at Naropa University, and Fine Art at the San Francisco Art Institute. Her work has been reviewed in many publications, including the *London Sunday Times* (Art and Culture), the *LA Times* and the *London Telegraph.* She was a presenter and writer on *The South Bank Show,* the UK's oldest and most respected arts program, and has presented programs on art, music and architecture for BBC TV, BBC World TV (Arts) and BBC Radio 6. She has written about art and culture for magazines such as *ID* and *The Face (UK),* and was a judge for the Sterling Prize. She now lives and works in the Bay Area.

Tom McGlynn is an artist, writer, and independent curator based in the NYC area. His work is represented in many national and international collections, including the permanent collections of the Whitney Museum, The Museum of Modern Art, and The Cooper-Hewitt National Design Museum of the Smithsonian. His art has been reproduced on the cover of *Artforum* magazine and featured in articles in *The New York Times.* Mr. McGlynn has taught as an Assistant Professor at Castleton State College, Vermont, and has previously been a Visiting Artist Lecturer at the Mason Gross School of Fine Arts at Rutgers University, NJ.

Throughout the '80s and '90s, **John Lurie** led the legendary band the Lounge Lizards. He recorded 22 albums and the soundtracks for over 20 films, including *Get Shorty*, which earned him a Grammy nomination. As an actor, he had starring roles in the Jim Jarmusch films, *Stranger than Paradise* and *Down by Law*, and supporting roles in Wim Wenders' *Paris, Texas*; Martin Scorsese's *The Last Temptation of Christ* and David Lynch's *Wild at Heart*, as well as a regular role on the HBO series *Oz*. Lurie wrote, directed and starred in the critically acclaimed television series, *Fishing with John*. For over thirty years, Lurie has been drawing and painting, yet only in the last eight years has he chosen to exhibit his work. In 2004, Lurie had his first painting exhibition at Anton Kern Gallery, New York. The Museum of Modern Art in New York and the Wadsworth Atheneum in Connecticut have acquired his work for their permanent collections. Lurie has published two collections of his work: *Learn to Draw*, a compilation of black and white drawings, and *A Fine Example of Art*, a full-color collection of over 80 reproductions. You can see more of his work, and buy prints, at johnlurieart.com.

Jenny Wade is a musician (her previous bands include Rude Buddha, Vodka, Swans and Timber) and has a Master's Degree in Russian Literature from Columbia University. She likes to translate the great Russian poets in the morning while having her tea. She lives with her husband and two daughters in California's Bay Area.

Chris Bava is an American photographer who lived and worked in Tijuana, Mexico. He was a former heroin trafficker who served 8 years in Federal prison following a worldwide sting operation in the late 1980s. Chris also struggled with addiction before and after his stint in prison, which eventually motivated him to move to Tijuana to seek out alternative cures. You can learn more about Chris and his fascinating life and work by watching a feature-length documentary, produced as part of the Exile Nation Project, available at: http://vimeo.com/38354777. He died in a car crash in October of 2012.

JD King is a graphic artist, experimental musician and writer living in upstate NY. Recent illustration clients include *The New York Times, The Boston Globe,* the US Postal Service, *Audubon Magazine, The Washington Post, The Baffler,* and *P.I.M.* His band, J.D. King & The Coachmen, have two high-energy avant-rock albums out on Ecstatic Peace.

Jose Padua has written poetry and fiction for in *Bomb, Salon.com, Exquisite Corpse, Another Chicago Magazine, Unbearables, Crimes of the Beats, Up Is Up, But So Is Down: New York's Downtown Literary Scene, 1974-1992*, and many other journals and anthologies. He has also written features and reviews for *NYPress, Washington City Paper*, the *Brooklyn Rail*, and the *New York Times*. He has read his work at the Lollapalooza Festival, CBGBs, the Knitting Factory, the Public Theater, the Living Theater, the Nuyorican Poets' Café, the St. Mark's Poetry Project, the Black Cat Club, the Washington Project for the Arts, and many other venues. He and his wife, the poet Heather Davis, are the authors of the blog Shenandoah Breakdown. They live with their daughter in Virginia's Shenandoah Valley.

Ted Barron has been making photographs and films since he was 12 years old and growing up in St. Louis. As a teenager he ran away and joined the circus. He soon found himself living in New York City which he has called home ever since. His work has been seen in numerous art and music publications including *Yeti* and *Bald Ego* as well as album covers by Steve Earle and Laura Cantrell. He edits and occasionally writes about music at the popular blog Boogie Woogie Flu (http://boogiewoogieflu.blogspot.com/), as well as maintaining his archive of photographs at Daily Pixel: Twenty-Ten (http://dailypixeltwentyten.blogspot.com/).

Eddie Woods (born May 8, 1940 in New York) is a writer, editor and publisher who lived and traveled in various parts of the world, both East and West, before eventually settling in Amsterdam, Holland, where in 1978 he started *Ins & Outs* magazine and two years later founded Ins & Outs Press.

John Farris is a long-time denizen of the Lower East Side—he still lives above the Bullet Space Gallery on East 3rd Street. He has been published in *Red Tape; Gathering of the Tribes; The Worst Book I Ever Read; Up Is Up, But So Is Down: New York's Downtown Literary Scene, 1974-1992; The Outlaw Bible of American Poetry* and *Let Loose on the World: Celebrating Amiri Baraka at 75.* His new novel, *The Ass's Tale* (Autonomedia) was published in September, 2010. "There is a hidden blessing in knowing John Farris, deeply hidden." —David Hammons

David de Biasio is an Italian painter born in Jesolo (Venice) on August 8 1973. His visual revelation took place in the United States, where he lived from 2003 to 2008, enriching his capacity for visual perception thanks to his contact with the variegated and lively New York arts scene and, above all, through his direct interaction with the original Photorealists. This experience led him to in-depth pictorial explorations aimed at achieving an extreme realism steeped in the Italian sense of Beauty.

Michael Carter published *Red Tape* magazine from 1980 to 1992. His work has been published in various Unbearables publications, *Between C & D* and *Peau Sensible*.

After being expelled from the art division of Bennington College, **Hal Hirshorn** went to Venice, Italy and came to New York where he completed his education in and around the city. He uses 19th century equipment and techniques to create found photographs of images whose original subject and meaning have been forgotten. His glossy prints are albumized salt prints that have been coated with a solution of egg whites, while the matte prints are created on plain salted paper. His work has been shown at Paris Photo, the Royal Academy in London and various other venues in London with Pierre Spake, the Association of International Photography Art Dealers with Thomas Harris in New York and the James Graham & Sons gallery in New York.

Wanda Phipps is a writer/performer living in NYC. Her publications and recordings include *Field of Wanting: Poems of Desire, Wake-Up Calls: 66 Morning Poems,* and the CD-Rom *Zither Mood*. Her poetry has been translated into Ukrainian, Hungarian, Arabic and Galician. She has received awards from the New York Foundation for the Arts, the National Theater Translation Fund, and others. As a founding member of Yara Arts Group she has collaborated on numerous theatrical productions presented in Ukraine, Kyrgyzstan, Siberia, and at La MaMa, E.T.C. in NYC. She's curated reading series at the Poetry Project at St. Mark's Church and written about the arts for *Time Out New York, Paper Magazine*, and *About.com*.

Norman Douglas was one of the original editors of *Peau Sensible*. He currently lives in Detroit, MI. You can find his musings and podcasts over at Individual Electric.

Ruby Ray got her start as staff photographer and muse at seminal punk culture rag, *Search & Destroy Magazine*, and co-founded *Re/Search Publications*; her iconic Burroughs photo graced the cover of issue 4/5. Ray's historic documentation of California's 1970s and 1980s underground music and art scene provides a rare insider's look at this pivotal time in musical history. A new hardback book, *From the Edge of the World, California Punk 77-81,* will be published in the Fall of 2012 and her Ebook is going to go live any day now on Amusedom: www.amusedom.com.

Rob Hardin is the author of *Distorture*, a callously florid collection of short stories that seduced the Firecracker Award into being won and then told the award it should really start seeing other people. His fiction and essays have manipulated their way into the anthologies *Avant-Pop: Fiction for a Daydream Nation*, *Postmodern Culture, In the Slipstream, Forbidden Acts, Storming the Reality Studio: A Casebook of Cyberpunk & Postmodern Science Fiction*, *Mississippi Review* and *An Exaltation of Forms*. As a studio musician, he has intimidated others into using him on more than forty albums.

Larissa Shmailo's work has appeared or is forthcoming in *Gargoyle, Barrow Street, Drunken Boat, Fulcrum, Rattapallax, Jacket, The Unbearables Big Book of Sex*, and the Penguin anthology *Words for the Wedding*. Her books of poetry are *In Paran* (BlazeVOX [books]), the chapbook *A Cure for Suicide* (Cervena Barva Press, with foreword by Philip Nikolayev), and the e-book *Fib Sequence* (Argotist Ebooks). Larissa recently won honorable mention in the international Russian literary translator's competition for the Compass Award sponsored by Princeton University; her original translation of A. Kruchenych's "Victory over the Sun" is archived at the Museum of Modern Art (MoMA), the Los Angeles County Museum of Art, and the Smithsonian, and may be read at the *Brooklyn Rail's* InTranslation site: http://intranslation.brooklynrail.org/russian/victory-over-the-sun. She blogs at http://larissashmailo.blogspot.com/.

Emily XYZ is an American writer and performer best known for her spoken-word poetry for multiple voices. Born in upstate New York, she moved to New York City in 1982 and was active in the downtown Manhattan performance art and music scene. In 1992 XYZ began working with actress Myers Bartlett. The pair has toured extensively in the U.S. and Canada as members of the seminal New York City spoken-word collectives The Nuyorican Poets Café Live! and Real Live Poetry, and on their own. A book and audio CD collection of XYZ's work for two voices, entitled *The Emily XYZ Songbook*, was published in 2004. Her poem "Slot Machine" was featured in the nationally broadcast Public Television [PBS] series The United States of Poetry. Her poems have also been published in several anthologies, including *Up Is Up, But So Is Down: New York's Downtown Literary Scene, 1974-1992*, and *Aloud: Voices from the Nuyorican Poets Cafe*. She is currently the Arts Queensland Poet in Residence.

Samoa Moriki was born in a small fishing town in Hiroshima, Japan. He has been a vital part of the art movement in downtown New York City since the early 80s, and is also known for being co-founder and guitarist of the legendary rock band, The Voluptuous Horror of Karen Black. He currently performs with the country-western band, The Lonely Samoans, and is available to paint portraits by commission.

Claiming home as North Carolina and working in Newark, NJ, **Joseph O'Neal** is an internationally collected artist and has been involved in numerous group and solo exhibitions in Miami, New York, Brooklyn, New Jersey, Philadelphia, Connecticut, California, Georgia, North Carolina, South Carolina, and Switzerland.

Jonathan Cowan was born on September 24, 1982 in Temple, Texas. He attended the University of Texas at San Antonio, where he received his Bachelor of Fine Arts in drawing in 2006. He currently lives and works in New York City.

Justin Clifford Rhody is a photographer based in Oakland, California. His work has been exhibited throughout the United States in small galleries & he has traveled extensively, presenting his work via slide projector in unconventional settings (such as warehouses, living rooms and backyards). His first book of photographs, *Sliding Glass Door,* was published in 2012. A monograph of photos from Central America titled *Zona Urbana* is slated to be published in the spring of 2015.

Charles Schick is a painter and an actor who appeared recently in several plays by Tennessee Williams. He's lived on New York's Lower East Side since 1981.

Jeff Spirer began photographing things at age ten. Although the casual observer might disagree, not much has changed in his photography since that time. He is interested in minimalist visions of world around him, as well as naked women and local rock stars striking iconic poses.

John S. Hall is an American poet, author and singer perhaps best known for his work with King Missile, an avant-garde band that he co-founded in 1986 and has since led in various disparate incarnations. He frequently writes and performs under the name-This Fuckin' Guy.

Rick Prol was born and raised in NYC where he currently lives and works. He graduated from

Cooper Union College in 1980 and began showing his work publicly in 1982, and curating group shows in 1983. He utilizes a language that is accessible and direct, but also filled with sly and knowing art historical references. Prol's aesthetic employs art brut expressionism to convey images of human folly and suffering in a variety of media including sculpture, installations, painting, drawing and writing.

Marina Loeb studied illustration at the Rhode Island School of Design and is currently a graphic artist living in San Francisco. Her work is often surreal and dark and is done in a graphic style that splices design and illustration. She works primarily as a freelance illustrator, but also sells prints of her work in online stores and gallery settings. Her personal work tends to address the human condition and rests on observations that compare human and animal behavior.

Clinton B. T. King, American, born 1976, lives and works in Brooklyn. Having graduated with an MFA in sculpture from The School of the Art Institute of Chicago Clinton King's has worked in an expansive array of materials and mediums with his most recent works manifesting in abstract painting. These works explore the tenuous boundaries between the creation of illusionistic space and an immediate response to the materiality of the painting medium and process. His work has most recently been exhibited at Transmitter (Brooklyn NY), The Dorsky Foundation (Brooklyn NY), One River Gallery Space (New Jersey), and Parallel Art Space (Brooklyn, NY). Previous exhibitions include Boots Contemporary Art Space (St. Louis, MO), Zaim Space (Yokohama, Japan), 1a Space Gallery (Hong Kong), Gallery 400 (Chicago, IL), Youkobo Art space (Tokyo, Japan), and The Suburban (Chicago, IL). He was recently selected for the Yaddo Artist retreat.

Julie Torres is a painter and arts organizer in NYC. Learn more about her work and projects at julietorres.weebly.com.

Daniel Kolm is a photographerand musician based in New York City. His photographs have appeared in *Public Illumination Magazine, Black Liquid* and The Unbearables anthologies,and on the cover of *The Plastic Factory* and *Divine Comedy,* both written by Ron Kolm. He is the lead guitarist and singer for the band Arklight, who have released countless cds and cassettes on labels across the US and overseas including Faux Pas Recordings and Phase! Records; they have played live in the bars and basements of Brooklyn and Queens.

Kym Ghee is a Los Angeles-based portrait photographer and writer. Over the last three years, Kym began experimenting with iPhoneography, when she realized the best camera is the one you have with you. The result is a painterly, moody body of work focusing on the city of angels, that has been displayed and published around the globe.

Leslie Hardie is an artist, illustrator and designer who works in the mediums of paint, charcoal, collage and pixels. She has exhibited her artwork widely and is currently collaborating with Robert Hardin on a book project.

After a career as photojournalist, **Jean-Christian Bourcart** (born in 1960 in Colmar, France) first gained attention in the art world for *Infertile Madonnas* (1992), a series of photographs taken in Frankfurt brothels that was widely exhibited and also published with an introduction by Nan Goldin. Other works include *Forbidden City* (1999), an investigation of swinging and S&M clubs shot with a hidden camera; *Traffic,* a study of commuters caught in traffic jams (2004); and *Sinon la mort* *te gagnait* (2008), an autobiography mixing text and photographs. In 2010, he shot his second feature movie, *Memories of the Days to Come,* a sci-fi thriller starring the award-winner Elodie Bouchez. In 2009, he documented Camden, NJ, which is one of the poorest and most dangerous cities in the U.S. Bourcart tried to understand and witness the real life behind the statistics. *Camden* was published by Images en Manoeuvre as a bilingual book, and won the Nadar prize for best book of photographs in France in November 2011. He has been living and working in New York since 1997.

Henner Schröder was born in West Germany in 1955, and raised in West Berlin. In 1977 he moved to the US to pursue art studies. After receiving BFA degrees in Printmaking and Sculpture from Mass College of Art, Boston (1983), Henner turned his focus on glass. In 1986 he earned his MFA degree, and in 1987 received a Fellowship at The Creative Glass Center of America. Since moving to Washington State, he has taught at the Pilchuck School, as well as Pratt Fine Art Center in Seattle. Currently he is the owner/operator of Vitroglyph Inc. glass casting studio in Chimacum. His work is represented in public and private collections in America, Asia and Europe.

Punk Art Surrealist **Winston Smith,** a master of "hand-carved" collage, has been crafting his thought-provoking art since the 1970's. Over the last 35 years, Winston has had numerous one-man shows in San Francisco, Los Angeles, New York City, London, Berlin, Antwerp, Rome and Tokyo. Smith first became known for his collaborations with punk legends Dead Kennedys. The "DK" logo that Smith created and designed for the band in early 1980 remains an intenational symbol of protest against authoritarianism. His images have also appeared in *The New Yorker, Playboy* and *Spin*, as well as numerous album and book covers. Winston's work is chronicled in three volumes of his collected works, *Act Like Nothing's Wrong* (Last Gasp, 1994), *Artcrime* (Last Gasp, 1999), and *All Riot on the Western Front* (Last Gasp, 2001).

Vladimir Mayakovsky (July 19, 1893–April 14, 1930) was a Russian and Soviet poet, playwright, artist and stage and film actor.

Liz Kresch is a Brooklyn native who tries to translate the vibrancy of everyday life into her work. Her influences are travel, music, film, friends, her daughter, memory, mystery and anything that strikes her as an image that could resonate on canvas. She studied art at the New York Studio School, Sarah Lawrence College and the Chatauqua Institute and kept eager and open to the passionate painters around her throughout her childhood and teen years. She cannot imagine life without the smell of turpentine.

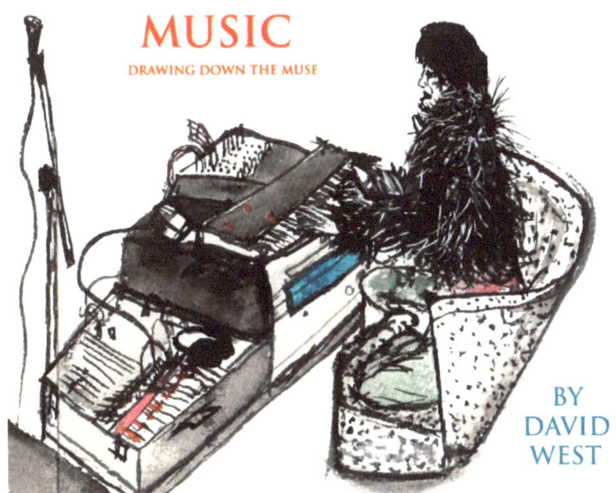

"Inside this book you get *portraiture vérité* of bands in action. Banging away in rehearsal. The appreciative eye watching the battle of the bands as they try to navigate their way through the sometimes complicated maze of illusions, delusions and solutions of grandeur before asphyxiation and evaporation of all the notes into the air. I'm the wrong person to comment on rehearsal as I work in a more backward way. I don't care if a performance is anally-retentive-perfect because a computer can do that now. I'll work hard on something to a point then I stop, as what I want surprises myself, especially in a live situation. It's a viewpoint probably not shared by most of the bands in this book but that's what makes things interesting. It's up to others to state theirs and that takes us to the artist.

"David West hits the target dead center BOOM with his beautifully liquid renderings of NYC bands in rehearsal. Mr. West captures a scene in the late 1990s largely ignored. These aren't vacuous American Idols but musicians who are The Real Deal. Like a fly on the wall, David gives you an inside view from his own multifaceted eye. There is a dripping aquatic fluidity to his drawings. Mr. West is not afraid to let the ink, gouache, and watercolor run and flow, never betraying the nature of his medium. That's why he's The Real Deal. If you the viewer can't understand, appreciate and see that in his work then go out and get corrective eye surgery!"

—Monte Cazazza of Psychic TV

Full Color Bleed on White paper | 8" x 7" | 110 pgs. | ISBN/EAN13: 0983927170 / 978-0983927174 | List: $24.95

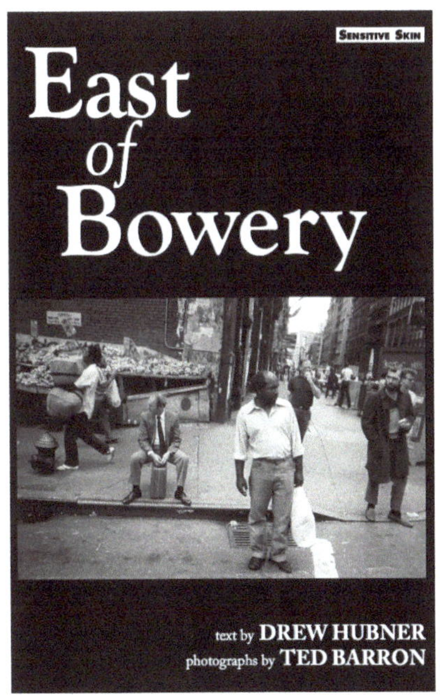

East of Bowery began as a collaborative web project between writer Drew Hubner (*American by Blood, We Pierce*) and photographer Ted Barron in 2008. It was subsequently performed as a multimedia performance with live musical accompaniment at The Gershwin Hotel and The Bowery Poetry Club. This is the first print publication of the project.

"Drew Hubner's prose and Ted Barron's photos are kin, at once raw and lyrical, grit and grace, which is what the city was like back then. The combination is magic, the essence of the time and place."

—Luc Sante, author of *Low Life* and *Kill All Your Darlings*

"*East of Bowery* is a sharply focused, street-level view of Downtown before the real estate agents started renaming everything."

—Steve Earle, author of *Doghouse Roses* and *I'll Never Get out of This World Alive*

"Drew Hubner writes like people used to."

—William Georgiades, *New York Magazine*

"The voice is loose, jazzy, and fast, the memories liquid and hot, avoiding the romance of macho drug memoirs with black humor, verisimilitude and a knack for the absurd."

—Kate Christensen, author of *In the Drink* and *The Astral*

Black & White on Paper | 6" x 9" | 154 pgs. | ISBN/EAN13: 0983927103 / 9780983927105| List: $15.95

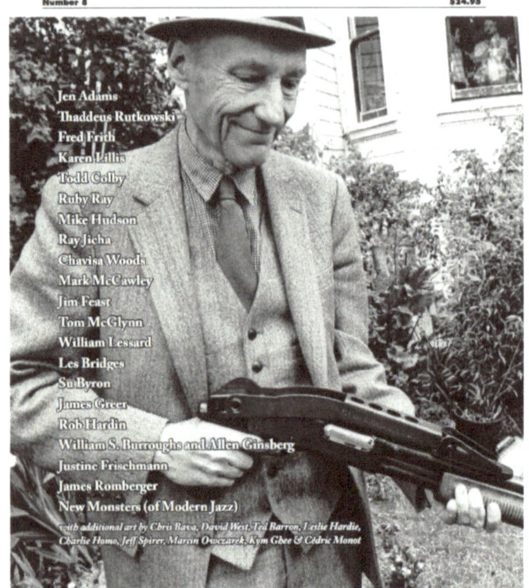

SENSITIVE SKIN #8

on sale at Amazon.com and select bookstores
PDF version available at sensitiveskinmagazine.com/downloads/sensitive-skin-8/

Featuring a rarely seen interview with **William S. Burroughs** by **Allen Ginsberg.**

With iconic punk photographs by **Ruby Ray**, art by **Tom McGlynn** and **Justine Frischmann**, music by **The New Monsters**, a comic written and drawn by **James Romberger**, writing by **Mike Hudson, James Greer, Thaddeus Rutkowski, Chavisa Woods, Jim Feast, Mark McCawley, Todd Colby** and much more.

Full Color on White Paper | 8.5" x 11" | 118 pgs. | ISBN-13: 978-0983927150 | ISBN-10: 0983927154 | List: $24.95

SENSITIVE SKIN #9

on sale at Amazon.com and select bookstores
PDF version available at sensitiveskinmagazine.com/downloads/sensitive-skin-9/

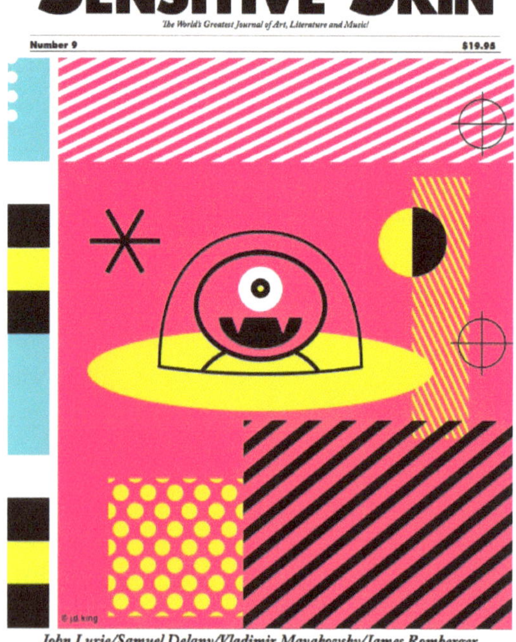

Featuring an exclusive interview with, and music by, seminal guitarist **Fred Frith** (Henry Cow) the missing chapter from the latest novel by science fiction legend **Samuel R. Delaney** and a portfolio of paintings from actor *(Stranger Than Paradise)* and musician (Lounge Lizards) **John Lurie.**

Plus a memoir by **Marty Thau**, former manager of Suicide and The New York Dolls, new translation of poetry by **Vladimir Mayakovsky** from **Jenny Wade,** photographs of the seamy side of Tijuana by **Chris Bava** and an interview with **Darius James,** conducted by **Ghazi Barakat**, about his new documentary, *The United States of Hoodoo.*

The front cover is by reknowned illustrator **JD King,** and the back cover features a comic written and drawn by **James Romberger.** There's more writing, by **Doug Rice, Susan Scutti, Larissa Shmailo, Bradley Spinelli, Anna Mockler, Jesus Angel Garcia,** and **Aman Sabet,** as well as art by **Ha Young Kim, Marcin Owczarek, John Griffin, David West** and **Justine Frischmann,** and photographs by **Ted Barron, Ruby Ray, Hal Hirshorn, N.D. Koster** and **Geoffrey Ithen.**

Full Color on White Paper | 8.5" x 11" | 102 pgs. | ISBN-13: 978-0983927167 | ISBN-10: 0983927162 | List: $24.95

SENSITIVE SKIN #10

on sale at Amazon.com and select bookstores
PDF version available at sensitiveskinmagazine.com/ downloads/sensitive-skin-10/

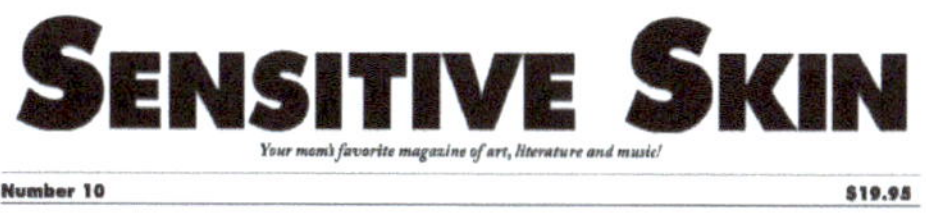

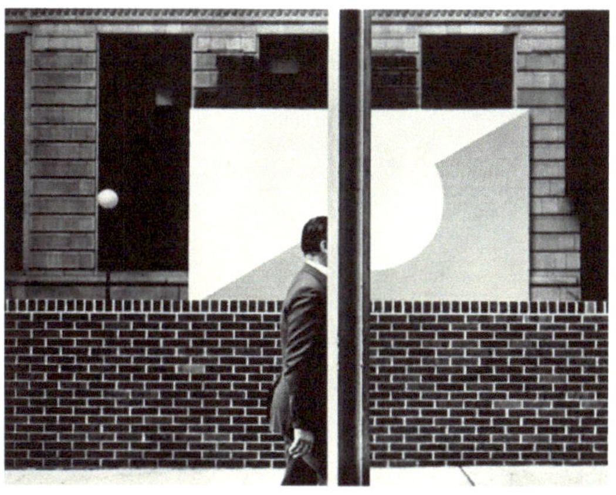

The issue features out-takes from the Wall Street collection by famed photographer **Charles Gatewood** (*Sidetripping, Forbidden Photographs*), fiction by downtown legends **Gary Indiana** (*Scar Tissue and Other Stories, White Trash, Horse Crazy, Gone Tomorrow*), **Max Blagg** (*Ticket Out*) and **Drew Hubner** (*East of Bowery*) plus work by Dead Kennedy's roadie and junky bankrobber **Patrick O'Neil** (*The Hold-Up*), radio host **Tony DuShane** (*Confessions of a Teenage Jesus Jerk*) newcomer **E.A. Fow** and South American novelist **Raul Serrano Sanchez** (*Catálogo de ilusiones*), with poetry by Flarf pioneer **Sharon Mesmer** (*Annoying Diabetic Bitch, The Virgin Formica*), **Ron Kolm** (*Divine Comedy*), **Pete Simonelli** (*Night Sees You First, A Lonely War*) and **Michael Randall**, essays by **James Reich** (*Bombshell; I, Judas*), **Ronald B. Richardson** (*Narrative Madness*), cinema of transgression co-founder **Nick Zedd** and South African activist **Breyten Breytenback** (*The True Confessions of an Albino Terrorist*). Includes paintings by **Peter Shear**, music by **Steve Adams** (ROVA Saxophone Quartet) and more.

Charles Gatewood/Gary Indiana/Sharon Mesmer/Nick Zedd/ Peter Shear/Patrick O'Neil/Max Blagg/Tony DuShane and much, much more…

Full Color on White Paper | 8.5" x 11" | 120 pgs. | ISBN-13: 978-0983927181 | ISBN-10: 0983927189 List: $24.95

SENSITIVE SKIN #11

on sale at Amazon.com and select bookstores
PDF version available at:
sensitiveskinmagazine.com/downloads/sensitive-skin-11/

SENSITIVE SKIN
Art, music and writing by and for people with ADHD, OCD, PTSD, LSD, OMG and WTF
Number 11 $24.95

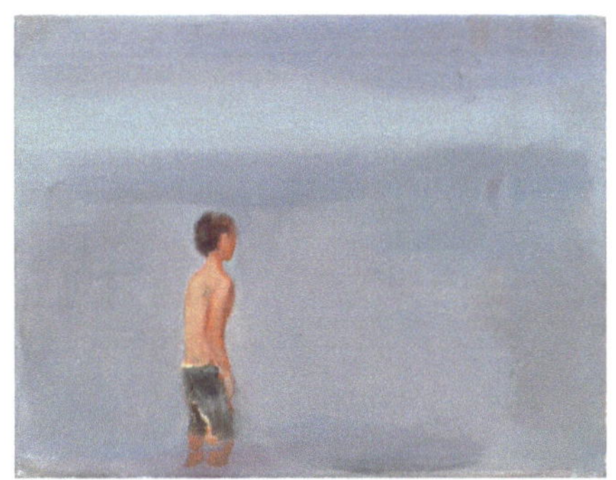

Maggie Estep/Alan Kaufman/Deborah Pintonelli/Stephen Lack

Features writing by **Arthur Nersesian** (*The Fuck-Up*), Spin columnist **Celia Farber, Maggie Estep** (*Diary of an Emotional Idiot, Hex, Alice Fantastic*), **D. Scot Miller** (*Knot Frum Hear*), **Deborah Pintonelli** (*Ego Monkey*), **Joshua Mohr** (*Damascus, Fight Song*), **Anonymous** (*Diary of an Oxygen Thief*), **Alan Kaufman** (*Drunken Angel, Matches*), **Marc Olmsted,** with an interview with **Dîre McCain,** editor of *Paraphilia Magazine*, by **Edward Robinson.**

We also have a great portfolio of paintings from East Village icon **Stephen Lack,** as well as photographs by **Gretchen Faust, Dennis Gordon** and **Evelyn Bencicova,** and live music from **Sun Ra,** recorded in NYC's Central Park in 1986.

Plus poetry by legend **Steve Dalachinsky** (*Fool's Gold*), **Sparrow, Lynn McGee, Rebecca Weiner Tompkins** (*Night Sees You First, A Lonely War*) and **Vladislav Khodosevic** (translated by **Jenny Wade**), an essay on post-collapse America as seen in *True Detective* by **Marian St. Laurent.**

Full Color on White Paper | 8.5" x 11" | 130 pgs. | ISBN-13: 978-0983927198 | ISBN-10: 0983927197 List: $24.95

www.ingramcontent.com/pod-product-compliance
Lightning Source LLC
LaVergne TN
LVHW070139110826
845147LV00002B/289

* 9 7 8 0 9 9 6 1 5 7 0 0 1 *